Four Faces of Jesus

The Uniqueness of the Gospel Narratives

Books by Leslie B. Flynn

The Four Faces of Jesus
How to Survive in the Ministry

LESLIE B. FLYNN

Four Faces of Jesus

The Uniqueness of the Gospel Narratives

Includes Built-in Study Guide for Personal or Group Study

kregel
PUBLICATIONS

Grand Rapids, MI 49501

The Four Faces of Jesus © 1993 by Leslie B. Flynn and published by Kregel Publications, a division of Kregel, Inc., P.O. Box 2607, Grand Rapids, MI 49501. All rights reserved.

Unless otherwise indicated, scripture quotations are from the Authorized King James Version. Those marked:

NIV are from *The New International Version of the Bible*, published by the Zondervan Corporation, © 1978 by the International Bible Society.

TLB are from *The Living Bible*, © 1973 by Tyndale House Publishers, Wheaton, IL.

PHILLIPS are from *The New Testament in Modern English* translated by J. B. Phillips, © 1972 by J. B. Phillips, published by the Macmillian Company, New York, N.Y.

Cover and Book Design: Alan G. Hartman

Library of Congress Cataloging-in-Publication Data
    The four faces of Jesus: the uniqueness of the gospel narratives / Leslie B. Flynn.
       p. cm.
    Includes bibliographical references and index.
    1. Bible. N.T. Gospels—Criticism, interpretation, etc.
2. Jesus Christ—Character. I. Title.
BS2555.2.F57   1993   226'.06—dc20   92-39333
                                                                                CIP

ISBN 0-8254-2638-3 (paperback)

    1 2 3 4 5 Printing / Year 97 96 95 94 93

Printed in the United States of America

Contents

Dedication

To My Grandchildren

Martin	Caroline
Guido	William
Christopher	Tara
(in heaven)	Sean
Jeremy	Casie
Amber	Jesse
Cori	Bobbi
Bobby	Nathan
Jimmy	Josie
Johnny	Dylan
Tommy	Sawyer

Foreword

W hen Universal Studios released the movie, *The Last Temptation of Christ* in 1988, Christian people across the USA protested what they considered a blasphemous attack against the Lord Jesus. The film downgraded the historical Jesus, making Him far less than the magnificent, all-glorious God-man pictured in the first four books of the New Testament.

The New Testament begins with four accounts of Jesus' earthly life. From the earliest centuries these narratives have been known as the four Gospels: Matthew, Mark, Luke, John. Gospel simply means "good news." Four writers relate the good news of Christ's incarnation, ministry, death and resurrection.

But why do we have four records?

Why four Gospels?

Why not just one single biography? Or two Gospels? Or three? Why not five records? Or twenty-three?

When giving a picture to a friend, we usually select ONE with a single view, invariably the most flattering pose.

Posters of the FBI's *Most Wanted* normally display TWO views of each criminal's face, both front and side.

On the same canvas in London's National Gallery are THREE

representations of King Charles I. On one side his head is turned to the left. On the other side, to the right. In the middle is a full-face view. Van Dyck painted all three to help a sculptor make a bust with a more accurate likeness of the king.

When it came time to describe in written form the richness of perfection displayed by Jesus during His thirty-three years on earth, the Holy Spirit inspired FOUR portraits which together were sufficient to provide a well-rounded delineation of His might, meekness, mercy, and majesty. Each Gospel films a distinctly separate aspect of His character.

To capture a specific trait of the Master, each author under the Spirit's direction exercised selectivity in the choice of words and deeds that would highlight the author's viewpoint. The photographing of the Master from four varying perspectives explains many of the variations in the four Gospels. Four of the following chapter titles, *Only in Matthew, Specially in Mark, Particularly in Luke, Uniquely in John,* emphasize the particular vantage point presented by each author, and show why certain items are included or omitted in certain Gospels.

For example, only in which Gospel occurs the phrase, "the kingdom of heaven"? And why?

Only which Gospel contains the word "immediately" or its equivalents "straightway" or "forthwith" approximately forty times, more than all the other three Gospels combined. Why?

Only which Gospel mentions an "only son" and an "only daughter"?

Which Gospel has the word "believe" ninety-eight times?

Only in which Gospel do we find the expression, "the lost sheep of the house of Israel"?

Which Gospel has many miracles but few parables?

Which Gospel speaks most about Jesus praying?

Only which Gospel contains the double "verily, verily"?

Wesley G. Pippert, a United Press reporter for thirty years, points out that secular journalists today produce stories that are very much alike. Embracing the same values, they write with similarity of perspective, concerned lest a different point of view puts them out on a limb. He writes, "Instead of fearing a variety of angles on a story, however, journalists should welcome diversity. The scriptures are a model in this regard. The four gospels contain essentially the same facts about Jesus, but are written from vastly different perspectives and to different audiences. The sum of these accounts is a multidimensional view of His life."[1]

Numerous accounts of Jesus' life existed. But the Holy Spirit inspired and safeguarded the variations of these four sketches to round out the manifold excellencies of the blessed God Who became perfect man. What practical value do these four differing portraits have for us today? This book shows how our Christian life may profit from reflections on the "four faces of Jesus."

1. *An Ethics of News*, Georgetown University Press, 1989, p. 24.

1

Four Views of
the Good News

E arly in my journalism training an editor explained the difference between a biographical sketch and a personality profile. In his thinking, a biographical sketch traces the main
chronological events of a person's life: birth, youth, education, marriage, family and career. But a personality feature delves more deeply
into an individual's psyche to see what makes him tick, and thus
discovers the leading personality characteristic(s) around which the
article should revolve. A biography follows the data of history, whereas a profile explores the traits of character.

INCOMPLETE BIOGRAPHY

The combined facts from all four Gospels fall notoriously short of
giving a complete biography of Jesus' earthly life. Though given a
few stories revolving around His infancy, the records omit the date of
His birth as well as any mention of His early education. The first
thirty years of His life are swathed in silence, except for a brief
episode in the temple when He was twelve. The Gospels major in

the approximately three-and-a-half years of His public ministry. During that period we can identify less than forty separate days on which He engaged in some activity. That means that, after a virtual silence of thirty years, we have biographical input on the average of around one day per month of those forty-two months of His public ministry.

Through the centuries harmonists have tried to reconstruct from the unarranged material of the Four Gospels an orderly life of Christ. The earliest recorded attempt at harmonization belongs to Tatian, pupil of Justin Martyr, who compiled the *Diatessaron* ("by means of four") around 160 A.D. Most harmonies historically have utilized a four-column synchronization. More recently, efforts have been made to blend the four Gospels into a single, chronological narrative. But though harmonies help position the Gospel events in correct time-place sequence, many details required for even a thumbnail sketch are notably absent. Huge gaps mar the completeness of the story.

FOUR PERSONALITY PROFILES

Matthew, Mark, Luke, and John did not set out to give a biographical sketch of the Lord Jesus. Therefore they did not document an exhaustive list of historical information. With facts somewhat meager and fragmentary we might expect our knowledge of Jesus to be inadequate and disappointing. But the reverse is true. Though much biographical data remains a mystery, sufficient facts enable us to grasp a clear picture of His character. The materials were not accidentally selected by whim of author recall, but were inspired by the Holy Spirit to give a four-sided portrait of God's incarnate Son. One account would not have been sufficient. All four were necessary to clearly delineate His multidimensional personality. Each writer features a distinct aspect of His character.

- Matthew paints Him as KING.
- Mark shows Him in the opposite role of SERVANT.
- Luke stresses His human side as MAN.
- John emphasizes His other side, as GOD.

Though each author pictures Him in all four aspects, each strongly accentuates just one of those distinctive areas. For example, Matthew depicts Jesus as servant, man and God, but makes His kingship his major emphasis. Likewise Mark, who highlights the servanthood of Jesus, also portrays His kingship, manhood and deity. Likewise, Luke, who delights in the human Jesus, does not neglect His deity; nor does John, who upholds Jesus as God, forget His humanity, recording, "Jesus wept" (11:35).

Would it not have been simpler if we had been given one clear, continuous, chronological account of Jesus' life, thus avoiding the difficulty of reconciling events vaguely positioned in time and place, and sometimes seemingly contradictory? Perhaps not. To try to mingle all four emphases into one such document would be confusing, as well as diminishing the distinctive flavor of each. One commentator equated the effort to amass all the Gospel facts into one harmony, while preserving the distinct emphasis of each, to an architect's attempt "to construct, from the materials of Solomon's temple, of the Parthenon, of the Coliseum, and of Westminster Abbey, a new temple which should preserve and harmoniously combine the peculiar features of them all, and be neither, Jewish, Greek, Roman, nor Gothic." [1]

C. I. Scofield, editor of the well-known *Scofield Reference Bible*, went so far as to say that the harmonized lives of Christ "serve to confuse the divine intent in the Four Gospels. They give a blur, and not a portrait. They have the effect of a composite photograph." Rather than writing a narrative biography, he says, "Four men inspired by the Holy Spirit, wrote four books, known as the Gospels, in which they presented the one Personality in His four great characters." [2]

SYMBOLISM

Students of biblical symbolism point out that four is the number of the earth: four points to the compass, four seasons of the year, four types of soil in Jesus' parable, and four world empires in Daniel's vision. How fitting, they suggest, to have four Gospels recounting the earthly ministry of the heavenly Savior.

Several Old Testament prophecies of the promised Messiah which give Him the title of Branch are amplified with an additional name. Significantly, these names coincide with the four portraits of Christ in the Gospels.

- "I will raise unto David a righteous Branch, and a King shall reign and prosper" (Jer. 23:5)—*King.*
- "I will bring forth my servant the BRANCH" (Zech. 3:8)—*Servant.*

1. Daniel S. Gregory, *Why Four Gospels*, Bible League Book Co., 1907, p. 14.

2. *Four Portraits of the Lord Jesus Christ*, George Soltau, Charles C. Cook, New York, *Foreword.*

- "Behold the man whose name is The BRANCH" (Zech. 6:12)—*Man.*
- "In that day shall the branch of the Lord be beautiful and glorious" (Isa. 4:2)—*God.*

Biblical scholars have pointed out the similarity between the symbolism of the four beasts around the throne (Revelation 4:7) and the four emphases of Christ in the Gospels. The parenthesis inserted after each beast explains its symbolism, "And the first beast was like a lion (KING), and the second beast like a calf (SERVANT), and the third beast had a face as a man (MAN), and the fourth beast was like a flying eagle (GOD)." These creatures in Revelation bear similarity to those in Ezekiel's vision (1:4-14). However, the order of appearance in Revelation is the same sequence as in the four Gospels: King (Matthew), Servant (Mark), Man (Luke), and God (John).

AUTHORS' QUALIFICATIONS

How were the four authors qualified for their tasks? What were their occupations? For what audience did each write? Though the four Gospels were intended ultimately for all people everywhere, each was likely aimed at a certain group.

Matthew wrote to the JEWS, perhaps pitching his account to the church at Jerusalem.

Mark had the ROMANS in mind. Likely he directed his volume to the church at Rome.

Luke penned his treatise to Theophilus, apparently a high official addressed as "most excellent." Luke seemed to point his narrative at the GREEKS and GENTILES.

John may have had the church at Ephesus in mind, but his purpose went far beyond to include the CHURCH EVERYWHERE, Jew, Roman and Greek, inviting whoever will.

Though all four Gospels were for the benefit of all men everywhere in all centuries, the Holy Spirit used each separate author to reach a certain class of readers with a specific emphasis. This emphasis determined the choice of materials.

Matthew

Matthew was the only writer who held an official position. He represented the Roman Empire as a tax-collector. He is the only author who presents Christ in an official relationship—the King of the Jews. Associated with the power of the Roman Empire, he wrote of the most powerful of realms—the kingdom of heaven.

As a tax-collector Matthew was adept at keeping accounts. His Gospel indicates that He maintained systematic records of both Jesus' short sayings and long discourses, including those that fulfilled Old Testament prophecies of a coming Messiah and King. As one of their race and well-versed in their Scriptures, he was well-fitted to present Christ to the Jews as fulfiller of the predictions contained in the law and prophets.

Since tax-collectors were despised as traitors by the Jews, Matthew experienced repugnance at the hands of his own people. Thus he was somewhat prepared to write of the opposition and hatred which Jesus experienced from His countrymen.

Mark

When I was a student at Moody Bible Institute, a question on an exam asked, "What were the occupations of the four Gospel writers?" Most students easily gave the correct answers for three of them. Matthew was a tax-collector; Luke, a physician; and John, a fisherman. But what was Mark? The teacher later read off a list of forty-six different answers given by the class, including electrician. Though every Jewish boy was taught a trade, the New Testament never reveals Mark's occupation.

However, we do know that Mark acted as a servant to Barnabas and Paul on their first missionary journey (Acts 13:5), when he doubtless performed many menial tasks. Because he deserted the enterprise, Paul refused to let him join his next missionary trip. But years later, after proving himself as a helpful servant, Mark was again wanted by Paul. A prisoner at Rome, Paul wrote Timothy, "Get Mark, and bring him with you, because he is helpful to me in my ministry" (2 Tim. 4:11, NIV). How fitting for servant Mark to present servant Jesus.

Roman readers, whom Mark had in mind, would have little or no interest in fulfilled prophecies and genealogies. When the good news advanced beyond the confines of Judaism, certain terms and expressions had to be omitted or altered. Alan Johnson, Wheaton College professor, participating in a dialogue of evangelicals and Jews, remarked, "Communication has to be contextually oriented. We learn by the paradigm of the New Testament itself. Each of the four Gospels has a different ethnic contextualization. And as the gospel went out of the Palestinian Jewish culture into other parts of the world, certain kinds of terminology were dropped because they did not have coinage in these communities." [3]

Roman readers would be deeply attracted to a man of service, action and deeds. A people of great energy, the Romans had conquered the known world through the exploits of legions of soldiers, who, like servants, had obeyed the orders of their commanding officers. This Gospel would appeal to the empire's large slave population. So Mark presents Christ as servant, reporting very few of His parables, but many of His miracles. His Gospel moves with electric rapidity and vigor, relating exploits rather than exposition.

Luke

The cultured Greeks passionately pursued the ideal of perfection. So Luke presents Jesus as the perfect man, superior to the corrupt Greek gods. Luke is perhaps the only Gentile among all the Bible authors (Col. 4:11-14). If so, how fitting that he should be selected to write to a Gentile audience.

As a doctor Luke shows astute understanding of human nature. By far, he gives the most material on the birth of Jesus, including several songs overflowing with joy at the event. He reports with compassion on the lowly, the needy, and the lost, and expresses no uncertain jubilation at the Savior's love for sinful men. He appeals to those of a sympathizing nature in his portrayal of the universal outreach of the gospel of grace.

John

Of the four Gospels, John is the deepest with its abstract discourses, thought-provoking dialogues, and profound prayers.

John terms himself "the disciple whom Jesus loved" (Jn. 21:20). He belonged to the inner circle with Peter and James, and may have been the most beloved. He reclined next to Jesus in the Upper Room, and standing close to the cross, was the one to whom Jesus entrusted the care of His mother. John was given an amazing grasp of spiritual truth, including the apocalyptic visions of Revelation.

---

3. "'Fulfilled Jews' or 'Former Jews'?" in *Christianity Today*, Oct. 7, 1988, p. 68.

He gives us the loftiest concept of Christ of all four Gospels. Whereas the other authors chiefly portray the outer life of Jesus, John penetrates to the holy of holies of Jesus' radiant personality. As the most intimate with Jesus of the Twelve, he was best fitted to present Christ as God.

Summarizing their styles, Matthew is *methodical*, building his account around the discourses of the King.

Mark is *pictorial*, displaying the rapidly moving activities of the Servant.

Luke is *narrative*, recording historical and humanitarian data in the life of the Son of man.

John is *intimate*, revealing in various conversations Jesus' unique position as the Father's Son.

SYNOPTIC PROBLEM

John's Gospel differs radically from the first three Gospels. Matthew, Mark, and Luke have so much in common in their historical approach to Jesus' life that they have been called the "Synoptic Gospels," or simply, the "Synoptics." The word "synopsis" comes from two Greek words "with" and "see," meaning a "view together" or a "collective seeing." Though Matthew, Mark, and Luke view Jesus' life from the same general vantage, distinct differences do exist. How to account for the difference in these three Gospels is what scholars term the "Synoptic problem." The questions of which author wrote first, of whether they depended on the writings of each other, or drew on some outside, mutual source of oral tradition, along with all the ramifications of these many theories, is a study too technical for this book. The main thrust of the following pages is to show how variations in all four Gospels fit the purpose of the four authors as each individually sketched Jesus' portrait.

AN EXAMPLE OF THE FOUR VARYING VIEWPOINTS

Here is the thesis of this book. As a building may be viewed from four different sides, so the Holy Spirit photographed the Lord Jesus from four varying viewpoints. Though He is the glorious subject of all four Gospels, each writer stressed a specific side of His personality, and so under inspiration selected materials that develop that particular trait. Later chapters will show why each writer included certain details and omitted others.

Many differences in the Gospels can be explained by the varying purposes of the writers. Authors often viewed Jesus from diverse angles, like two knights who fatally wounded each other in a fight over whether a shield was bronze or gold. Both were right, for one side was bronze, and the other gold. But approaching from opposite sides, each saw a different metal. Close examination of many Gospel accounts show them not contradictory, but complementary. Experts in jurisprudence remind us that if witnesses use precisely the same words on the witness stand, we suspect coaching and collusion. Differing but reconcilable accounts in the Gospels raise our confidence in the authors' credibility.

At this point we cite one example of differing approaches by the four authors to the same event: the genealogies of Jesus at the beginning of the Gospels.

THE GENEALOGIES

Which of the Gospels begin with genealogies? Matthew and Luke. But not Mark. John has a prologue which more or less serves as a genealogy. The inclusion or omission of a genealogy provides a striking instance of why the four authors selected their respective materials.

Matthew

How logical for Matthew, who presents Jesus as King, to begin with a genealogy. Does not a king have to prove his right to the throne by succession? A king comes to rule by birth, not by ballot. So Matthew introduces his Gospel, "The book of the generation of Jesus Christ, the son of David, the son of Abraham" (1:1). God promised David a son who would sit on His throne forever (2 Sam. 7:8-13). Matthew traces Jesus' ancestry through David to prove His royal descent and right to the throne of Israel. And, because Jesus is the King of the Jews, Matthew traces His lineage back only to Abraham, the father of the Jews.

Mark

Mark has no genealogy. His story opens with Jesus already an adult. Why no genealogy? Because he accents Jesus as servant! No employee has to produce his pedigree to qualify for employment. Though I have held many jobs in my life—delivering a paper route, marking the board in a stockbroker's office, stenographing in an office, writing continuity for a radio station, bussing dishes in a dining-room, clerking behind a meat counter, and pastoring church-es—I have never been asked to show my genealogy.

In presenting Jesus as servant Mark had no need to prove any ancestral nobility; hence, no lineage.

Luke

Since Luke features Jesus as man, he gives us His ancestry all the way back to the first man.

Wouldn't it seem unnecessary to prove the manhood of Jesus by tracing his family tree back to Adam? Wasn't it clearly evident that Jesus was a human like us, though without sin? Strange as it may seem, some early cults considered Jesus more of a celestial ghost, denying His humanity. An early heresy, Docetism (from the verb "to seem"), claimed Jesus was not a real man, but a spectral appearance. He just "seemed" to suffer for humanity's sins, for how could a divine phantom possibly die? To many the idea of God becoming flesh came off as nonsense.

Another heresy of the early centuries, Gnosticism, believed ultimate deity could have no contact with matter, which they considered evil. To keep God distant from the material world, they explained creation by a series of emanations or aeons, which they interposed between God and His creation. They claimed that Jesus was one of these aeons, possessing no body at all. He was a clever hallucination, making Him a sort of heavenly ghost. So we see why Luke includes a genealogy of Jesus Christ which traces Him back to Adam (Luke 3:38)—to prove His genuine humanity. We also understand why the New Testament points out the heresy of denying that Jesus Christ came in the flesh (2 John 7). Jesus is the second Adam, Who came bodily to rescue us from the sin of the first Adam.

John

John presents Jesus as God. Since God doesn't have a genealogy, John omits one. God didn't send His Son into the world to become His son, for He always was God's Son.

Jesus had no beginning. As the eternal Son He existed before all things (1:1). Uncreated, He created all things. Then at a time in history He became flesh and dwelt among us for thirty-three years (1:14), revealing what God was like.

John's prologue (1:1-18) contains a virtual genealogy in its lofty statement of Jesus' pre-creation pedigree, especially summed up in the opening and closing sentences, "In the beginning was the Word, and the Word was with God, and the Word was God . . . And the Word was made flesh, and dwelt among us."

This book is divided into six sections of two chapters each. The opening section is introductory. This initial chapter states the thesis that the four Gospels photograph the Lord Jesus from four differing viewpoints. The second chapter turns attention to how the Gospels begin—with a genealogy (Matthew 1:1-17)—and shows how a seemingly dull list of names gives a strong hint of the grace Jesus will exercise during His earthly ministry.

Then follows four sections, each one devoted to a Gospel in their New Testament order: Matthew, Mark, Luke, and John. The first chapter in each section illustrates the vantage point of that particular author, explaining why certain items are included, and others excluded. The second chapter in each section aims to apply the lesson of that Gospel's portrait of Jesus' personality.

The sixth and final section deals with two central concepts that appear in all four Gospels.

IN ALL FOUR GOSPELS

Remarkably few episodes occur in all four Gospels. For example, no parable is related in all four. The only miracle recorded in all four is the feeding of the five thousand. Even birth accounts are not found in all four. Not till we reach the events revolving around Jesus' death do we find mention by all four. This is not surprising when we recall the purpose of His coming to earth. He came to die. Or as He Himself put it, "Even as the Son of man came not to be ministered unto, but to minister, and to give His life a ransom for many" (Matt. 20:28).

This explains why all four Gospels center on the final week of Jesus' life, devoting nearly a third of their writings to those few days. The gospel, Paul declared, was "that Christ died for our sins according to the Scriptures; and that He was buried, and that He rose again the third day according to the Scriptures" (1 Cor. 15:3, 4). Not till the so-called triumphal entry into Jerusalem which we celebrate on Palm Sunday do we find many incidents common to all four writers, such as Judas' betrayal, Peter's denial, Jesus entering Gethsemane, His arrest, trial before Pilate, crucifixion at the place of a skull with two others, burial by Joseph of Arimathaea, and the resurrection.

- The King dies and rises.
- The Servant dies and rises.
- The Son of Man dies and rises.
- The Son of God dies and rises

The essential, central facts around which Matthew, Mark, Luke, and John arrange their material and which makes their messages GOOD NEWS, and to which His incarnation and ministry led, are simply His death on the cross where He became the sacrifice for our sins, and His triumphant rising on the third day. Matthew, Mark, Luke, and John did not have four separate Gospels. All four penned the same Gospel, which Paul stated thus—He "was delivered for our offences, and was raised again for our justification" (Rom. 4:25). This is the old, old story which ever remains the glad, good news.

The two final chapters in this book will deal with the death and resurrection of Jesus Christ. One looks at the cross from the standpoint of Barabbas, who is mentioned in all four Gospels. The other deals with His mighty victory over the grave, the climactic event of all four records.

The King, rejected at His first coming, will one day return to this earth in glory to be honored as King of Kings.

The faithful Servant, now at God's right hand, is still working with and through His faithful servants on earth.

The Son of Man still understands our sorrows, and sympathizes with us in our troubles.

The Son of God has returned to His Father to prepare a place for those who love Him and abide in His Word.

A preacher announced a meeting at which people could voice their objections to Christianity. Hundreds were present. One man said, "The church is a rich man's club." Another objected to the hypocrites in the church. The pastor wrote down each complaint. When the congregation had finished, the pastor rose, "Friends, you have listed 27 objections. You have objected to church members, to pastors, to the Bible, and to many other things, but you have not said one word against my Master!" Then in a few simple sentences he spoke about the sinless, stainless, faultless Christ, inviting them to put their trust in Him.

Together, the four Gospels present the perfect Person, fully God and fully man.

2

How the Gospels Begin:
The Gospel in
the Genealogy

On my father's side I can trace my ancestry back only two generations to Ireland. But on my mother's side I can track my lineage back 300 years to a progenitor born around 1700 in Germany. Because of political wars, his family sought refuge in England, and were eventually shipped to the new America just fifty years before the colonists launched the War of Independence. Out of appreciation to England, my branch of the family emigrated from New Jersey to Canada, where they were known as United Empire Loyalists, and given a grant of land by His Majesty's government in 1795. For years my ancestral tree hung on a wall in Dundurn Castle in Hamilton, Ontario, till transferred to the basement of nearby Dundas Museum. I recall, as a boy, gazing at this tree, noting my spot on a lower limb, proudly aware of my heritage.

Interest in genealogical research received a boost through the TV series, *Roots,* in which a black American tracked his origin to the very village in Gambi, Africa, from which his forefather had been captured and shipped as a slave to America.

Suggestions abound for those who wish to ferret out their beginnings. Start in the attic, gathering old boxes of photos, diaries, letters, birth certificates and family Bibles. Jot down old family stories. Search county offices for deeds of lands and houses, military records, and grave markings. Genealogical magazines often provide clues. One amateur genealogist quipped, "It's like a detective story except that you don't get shot."

Some discoveries may bust our buttons with pride. A friend claims that he can trace his lineage to the seventeenth century, all sea-captains with the same last name. Blue bloods must beware of bragging, like the lady who asked, "Our family goes back to George Washington. How far does yours go back?" Came the deflating reply, "Don't know. They were lost in the flood."

On the other hand, the curious may not always like what they find. One social climber paid a researcher $500 to dig up her family tree. Learning of a black sheep among her forebearers, she immediately offered the researcher another $500 to bury the tree and keep quiet! A lawyer, who discovered that an ancestor had been hanged for cattle-stealing rewrote, "Great grandpa died while taking part in a public ceremony—when the platform gave way."

The Bible contains numerous genealogies. The relentless parade of passing generations reminds of the brevity of life and the certainty of death. Inexorably time marches on, "one entombed as another enwombed."

To the ancient Jew genealogies were important. For example, no man could serve as a priest in Israel unless able to show his descent from Aaron. Paul proudly traced his to Benjamin. But usually we find the genealogies bewildering. When President Eisenhower's mother urged him to read the Bible through, she excused him from wading through the "begats." Many of us skip over or skim through them. But one lady who spent years memorizing various biblical genealogies explained, "On arrival in heaven I would like to know who is related to whom!"

The four Gospels begin with a genealogy. Matthew devotes the first seventeen verses of his book with a listing of Jesus' ancestral line. What purposes does this lineage have, right up front in the New Testament?

IT INTRODUCES THE FOUNDER OF A NEW FAMILY

Interestingly, both Old and New Testaments begin with a striking similarity—a genealogy. Genesis 5:1 reads, "This is the book of the generation of Adam." Matthew 1:1 starts, "This is the book of the generation of Jesus Christ." God's dealings with earth's people revolve around these two households. The first Adam, into whose family all of humanity is born, sinned and dragged the race down. Because we are all Adam's sons and daughters, our world finds itself in its present predicament.

But God chose to do something about it. He sent His Son, made of a woman and descendant of a long lineage, to enter the human family to start a new household. He became partaker of lost humanity that members of a fallen family might become heirs of God's family. Through Jesus Christ we can transfer into the family of God—a supernatural regeneration—which makes us children of God. The genealogical record at the opening of the New Testament introduces the founder and head of this new family.

IT ESTABLISHES JESUS' RIGHT TO THE THRONE OF DAVID

For centuries the Jews had anticipated the birth of their Messiah-King. God chose the family line of Abraham and the household of King David as the channel through which His Son would enter the world. How logical for the first verse of the New Testament to state that Jesus was a descendant of David, Israel's greatest king, and also of Abraham, father of the Jewish race. To prove Jesus' right to the throne of Israel Matthew outlined Jesus' ancestry. Who cares about the pedigree of servants, but the parentage of kings counts for everything.

Luke also contains a genealogy, which differs somewhat from Matthew's. Matthew's descends through history from past to present, from father to son, repeating the verb "begat." But Luke's ascends from the present back through past centuries, from son to father, repeating the phrase, "was the son of." Since Matthew presents Jesus as King of the Jews, He goes back only to Abraham, prime patriarch of the Jews. Because Luke portrays Jesus as perfect Man, he traces back to Adam, father of mankind.

Though harmonization of the two accounts has its difficulties, many Bible scholars hold that Matthew gives Joseph's line, and

Luke gives Mary's side of the family. Bible scholars also point out the significance of the virgin birth. Had Joseph been Jesus' biological father, Jesus could not have occupied the throne because of the curse on the royal line from the days of Jeconiah (Jer. 22:30; Matt. 1:11). Restating, Matthew seems to follow the legal lineage through Joseph, while Luke handles the natural descent through Mary.

IT ILLUSTRATES THAT A PERSON'S CHARACTER IS NOT NECESSARILY DETERMINED BY HEREDITY

Classes in child education always debate the relative merits of heredity and environment. Which is more powerful: parentage or training? Do good parents always produce good children? And are the offspring of evil parents always doomed to turn out evil? Seventeenth century Thomas Fuller found the genealogy of Jesus strangely checkered with four remarkable changes in four immediate generations. He listed them as follows (vs. 7, 8):

(1)   Rehoboam, a bad father, begat Abia, a bad son.
(2)   Abia, a bad father, begat Asa, a good son.
(3)   Asa, a good father, begat Jehosophat, a good son.
(4)   Jehosophat, a good father, begat Joram, a bad son.

Fuller commented "I see, Lord, from this, that my father's piety cannot be handed on; that is bad news for me. But I also see the actual impiety is not always hereditary; that is good news for my son." This genealogy demonstrates that heredity cannot invariably determine the goodness or perversity of the next generation.

IT IS A CRYPTIC MESSAGE AS TO THE PERFECTION OF THE PROMISED KING

Close scrutiny reveals the incompleteness of the genealogy. Fewer names are found than in David's complete line listed in the books of Kings and Chronicles. Sufficient data did exist for Matthew to pen a complete and precise genealogy, had he been so inspired. Because of omissions in the record, we must conclude that he must have had in view some purpose other than striving for comprehensive historical accuracy.

The arrangement of the names into three widely differing periods, each with the same number of generations, indicates that Matthew did not purpose an inerrant pedigree. Rather, he deliberately left out some of Jesus' ancestors in order to round out three cycles of fourteen generations each: 1,000 years from Abraham to David, 400 years from David to the Babylonian captivity, and 600 years from the Babylonian captivity to the birth of Jesus. He was giving a cryptic message that pointed to the worth of the baby who possessed this genealogy.

Matthew's arrangement emphasized the numbers three and fourteen. Bible numerologists suggest the following significance. Seven stands for perfection. Since two stands for confirmation (two witnesses required for attestation), fourteen is double perfection. With the number fourteen repeated three times, the idea of perfection is intensified. Since three stands for the Godhead, Jesus' divine nature is indicated. To build his numerical cryptogram Matthew had to omit several names in Jesus' background. By sacrificing genealogical exactness he aimed to convey the perfection and deity of King Jesus, as well as His human descent through David and Abraham.

It Foreshadows the Merciful Nature of His Coming Ministry by Including the Names of Four Unlikely Women

Wouldn't you think that Matthew would have included only those ancestors of the finest pedigree, those of which Jesus would have been proud to have in his family? It's no surprise to find some of Israel's greatest heroes featured: Abraham, Isaac, Jacob, David, and Solomon. And all ranks of life are included, kings and commoners, rich and poor. Strangely, some blatantly evil men are listed, like Manasseh, perhaps the most wicked king to reign over the southern kingdom.

But what does cause astonishment is the gratuitous appearance of four women, especially some of dubious and even unsavory quality. The writer could have easily traced the genealogy without mentioning these characters whose names were unnecessary and irrelevant to the onflowing of history. Yet these four women are added in. Why? To display the deep-quality mercy which the Lord Jesus would exercise in His coming ministry. Their inclusion was a foreshadowing of the good news He would bring, and has been called the Gospel in the Genealogy.

- "Judas begat Phares and Zara of Thamar" (Tamar) (vs. 3),
- "Salmon begat Booz of Rachab" (Rahab) (vs. 5),

- "Booz begat Obed of Ruth" (vs. 5),
- "David begat Solomon of her that had been the wife of Urias" (a reference to Bathsheba) (vs. 6).

What do the lives of these four women: Tamar, Rahab, Ruth, and Bathsheba tell us about the good news?

THE GOSPEL EXTENDS TO WOMEN

Only male names were usually listed in Jewish genealogies, reflecting the non-status of women. Jewish boys learned to give thanks "for not being born an idolater, slave or a woman." In many parts of the world today women count for little, as soldiers in the Desert Storm War discovered.

A few years ago on a trip to mission fields, I discovered that, for the most part, women in West Pakistan were secluded. When they did venture outside, they wore burkas, which resembled long lampshades, extending almost to the ground, fitted with slits for eyes and mouth, all reminiscent of a masquerade. When I asked a wealthy man how many children he had, he said four, only reluctantly admitting to having three daughters. Learning I had seven daughters, out of genuine pity he gave me a gift. On the same trip, invited by a grandmother into her open-air apartment along with my wife and a missionary doctor, I was called names by a teenage boy who threatened to stone me because I had trespassed the forbidden territory of a women's residence.

The inclusion of four women in the line of Jesus in a day noted for its male chauvinism grabs our attention. A revolutionary and astonishing change was about to take place. The coming Messiah would gather women about Him, giving them an honorable place in His kingdom. It wouldn't be so much what He said, but how He related to women. They would feel at ease in His presence like the much-married Samaritan woman, also the two women who took down their hair to dry His feet, an unheard of practice. No rabbi would have entered the home of two unmarried sisters like Mary and Martha. Women would accompany Him in His travels from time to time, even supporting Him financially (Luke 8:1-3). Women would be last at the cross and first at the tomb.

This openness to womanhood would carry over into the New Testament church. In the last chapter of Romans Paul lists the names of about 27 friends, one-third of whom are women. Phoebe,

Priscilla, Lydia, Euodias, and Syntyche are but a few of Paul's fellow-workers. Women have been active in Christian service through the centuries. Because women often outnumber men on the mission field, and because of the generous legacies of well-to-do men, someone quipped that missionary work has been mostly carried on by living women and dead men.

The genealogy anticipated Paul's later important statement that in Christ "there is neither male nor female" (Gal. 3:28).

THE GOSPEL INCLUDES GENTILES

As God's chosen people, the Jews were commanded to maintain separation from other nations. Intermarriage with Gentiles brought on divine judgment, culminating in captivity. Aware of warnings against heathen fraternization, we are surprised to find Gentiles among Jesus' progenitors. All four women in His genealogy have Gentile connections.

Tamar, wife of Er, Judah's firstborn (Gen. 38:6, 7), was likely a Gentile. Says the *Pulpit Commentary*, "She is not expressly called a Canaanite, though it is more probable she was. Commentator Lange conjectures that she may have been of Philistine descent. . . ." [1]

Rahab, who hid the spies and was later rescued from her city of Jericho, was undoubtedly a Canaanite (Joshua 2; 6:25).

Bathsheba, not specifically named in the genealogy, is identified as Solomon's mother and "Uriah's wife" (1:6 NIV). Whether or not Bathsheba was a Gentile, she was linked to a Gentile husband, "Uriah, the Hittite" (2 Samuel 11:3).

Ruth, a Moabitess whose nation had troubled Israel for generations, presents an emphatic example of pagan background in the Savior's lineage. In Moab to escape the famine back in Bethlehem, and bereft of husband and sons, embittered Naomi decided to return home on hearing conditions were better. When daughter-in-law Ruth wanted to accompany her, Naomi tried to dissuade her. But Ruth insisted on joining her, uttering a declaration of loyal devotion, including the vow, "thy people shall be my people, and thy God my God" (Ruth 1:16). Ruth counted the cost of leaving her country, and the prospect of permanent widowhood. She chose

---

1. (Genesis, p. 441, Funk & Wagnalls Co., new edition, no date).

to forsake her heathen heritage, reject the idols of Moab, and find refuge in the God of Abraham.

Her faith was richly rewarded. In divine providence she married a close relative of Naomi, becoming the great grandmother of David, and thus a forebear of the King. Little did she know her story would become a book of the Bible, bearing her name. The lineage from Tamar to David given in Ruth 4:18-22 is identical with the comparable record in Matthew 1:3*b*-6*a*.

The inclusion of Gentile women in Jesus' genealogy anticipates the universal invitation of the Gospel. John the Baptist called Jesus the Lamb of God that "taketh away the sin of the world" (Jn. 1:29). Early in His ministry Jesus said that "many shall come from the east and west and shall sit down with Abraham, and Isaac, and Jacob, in the kingdom of heaven" while the children of the kingdom would be cast out (Matt. 8:11, 12). The well-known John 3:16 proclaims that God so loved the world. The Great Commission told the disciples to go into all the world and make disciples of all nations. In heaven, praises will be sung to the Lord Jesus Christ, sounding and resounding from the redeemed of every kindred, tongue, people and nation (Rev. 5:9).

An American missionary on the island of Madagascar wrote my wife, "I am awed at how God works. My Indian daughter-in-law, saved from Hindu background in Kenya, is using lessons on 'Women of the Bible' I prepared in Madagascar for Malagasy women, to teach Chinese teens in America."

THE GOSPEL EMBRACES SINNERS

Matthew does not single out the better known, exemplary women like Sarah, Rebekah, and Rachel, but chooses some who are not only Gentile, but who are also flagrant violators of the commandment prohibiting adultery. Three of them carry sexual stigma. Tamar was guilty of incest. Rahab was a prostitute. Bathsheba was guilty of marital infidelity. God produced the Savior from a line containing some unsavory people. As a cowboy graphically phrased it, "God grows roses out of horse manure."

Tamar

Chapters 38 and 39 of Genesis pose a stark contrast. In 39 Joseph heroically withstood the repeated seductive propositioning of Potiphar's wife. In the previous chapter Judah violated his own daughter-in-law, Tamar, who had married his oldest son. When his son died, Judah sent Tamar packing to her father's house, promising to give her a husband later. When she saw this unlikely to happen, Tamar tricked Judah into adultery by disguising herself as a prostitute, and sitting along his route. Pregnant, and liable for stoning, Tamar produced Judah's staff and signet which he had given her as a pledge, identifying him as the culprit. He acknowledged the obvious. Twins were born.

What Tamar did was dishonorable, but typical for a pagan girl resorting to the practices of her culture. Perhaps God honored her desire to be included in the family of God. We read, "Judas begat Phares and Zara of Thamar" (1:3). Immoral by biblical standards, she is found in Jesus' genealogy—along with the Virgin Mary.

Rahab

Almost every time Rahab is mentioned in the Bible she is identified by her disreputable profession—a harlot. She risked her life by hiding two strangers from Israel. Already aware of God's power in protecting Israel, she learned more about Jehovah from the two spies. To spare herself and family in the coming attack on Jericho she was told to bring them all into her house, and hang a scarlet thread from the window. Later she was graciously welcomed into the Jewish community, claimed as a bride in marriage, and amazingly became a link in Jesus' line.

The writer of Hebrews lists many heroes of faith like Abraham, Isaac, Jacob, and Moses, then adds, "By faith the harlot Rahab perished not with them that believed not, when she had received the spies with peace" (11:31). Cleansed from her sin and no longer Rahab the harlot, she became a member of God's *Who's Who*, prefiguring the forgiving nature of the coming Messiah.

Bathsheba

Though not mentioned by name, she is identified as the wife of Uriah whom one day David saw bathing, and called for. Refusing the summons of a king may have been difficult, yet Bathsheba shared guilt in the act of adultery. When she informed the king of her pregnancy, he concocted a plan to blame her husband. Thwarted, David virtually ordered Uriah's death by having him positioned in the "forefront of the hottest battle." A year later David poured out his heart in confession to God. Bathsheba doubtless asked for divine pardon. Though the baby died, God later blessed them with the birth of Solomon. Again, the genealogy shows grace.

How could three sinful women find their way into Jesus' pedigree? The answer lies in the cross where Jesus died to save sinners. Nothing in their lives merited divine favor. Pure, sovereign, matchless grace embraced these women. The stream of forgiveness flows from the very start of the New Testament.

PREVIEW OF THE GOSPEL

Jesus' genealogy forecasts the wideness of God's mercy. His forbearance included women, Gentiles, and sinners. The good news proclaims Jesus as the friend of both genders, kinsman to all races, and Savior of every penitent.

As we read the Gospels, we are not surprised to find Jesus accused of keeping company with sinners. He called Matthew, compiler of this genealogy and a sinner-publican, to be one of the Twelve. He brought salvation to Zacchaeus, chief publican of Jericho, who had become rich through cheating. He promised paradise to the dying thief. He welcomed harlots and publicans above Pharisees who prided themselves on both their self-righteousness and ancestry to Abraham. He comforted the woman caught in adultery, "Neither do I condemn thee: go, and sin no more." His loving kindness reflects most thoroughly in His dealing with the Samaritan woman. She was feminine. She was a despised Samaritan. She was living in immorality.

Diamonds come from carbon, which also gives us coal and ashes. Jesus can take the cinders of a life on the scrap heap, and make the derelict a sparkling jewel. "Christ Jesus came into the world to save sinners" (1 Tim. 1:15). Perhaps the little girl wasn't too far wrong when she misquoted that verse, "Christ Jesus came into the world to save cinders."

A seemingly dull genealogy on the first page of the New Testament flashes with gleams of grace. He whose ancestors were sinful will adopt repentant sinners into His family, make God their Father, while He Himself becomes their Elder Brother.

3

Only in Matthew

A skillful driver, heading home through the streets of Los Angeles at twilight, approached an avenue beyond which was a steep climb. Not wishing to shift gears, he jockeyed for a running start as he approached the intersection. On the left, the avenue was clear. But on the right, two fairly close cars were nearing the corner. Realizing that he could not beat the first car, he thought that he could slip through the space between the two vehicles, and maintain his momentum. He stepped on the gas to shoot into the opening between them. The driver had judged correctly. He had just enough room to slip comfortably between the two cars. But just as he darted through, to his consternation he spotted something he had failed to see in the dusk. The first car was towing the second one. They were fastened together by a steel cable. Weeks later, recuperating from his injuries, the driver pondered the truth that you cannot cut between two things that are bound together. Like those cars, the Old and New Testaments are closely hitched by prophecy and fulfillment. As it is often said, "In the Old Testament the New is contained, and in the New Testament the Old is explained."

Matthew is the book that bridges the two Testaments. Standing at the beginning of the New Testament, Matthew breaks the long 400-

year silence at the end of the Old Testament, and serves as the connecting link between the two. The Old Testament had closed with Israel looking for its long-promised Messiah and King. Matthew shows that Jesus was that King. The message of the Old Testament could be summed up, "He will come!" Matthew now resounds, "He is here! Joy to Israel and to the world! The King has come! We have found Him, of whom Moses and the prophets did write, Jesus of Nazareth!"

Three major characteristics describe the Gospel of Matthew: *Jewish, Topical, Kingly.*

JEWISH

On page after page Matthew links his Gospel with the Old Testament by demonstrating that ancient prophecies have been fulfilled in the person of Jesus Christ. Matthew refutes the misconception that a Jew must give up his Old Testament roots on espousing Jesus as the Messiah. On the contrary, a Jewish Christian merely surrenders the shadows and types of the Old Covenant for the substance and reality of the New Covenant.

A Jewish lady who became a believer in Jesus tells of her initial struggle. "I only knew that I wanted to find out the truth about Jesus and that I trusted God to show me. I began to wonder about the New Testament. I wanted to read it, but was afraid. I didn't want the disapproval of those I loved. Yet I was so curious to read that book. I'd seen it in the Newberry's 5 & 10. I knew how much it cost, and I wanted it very badly. I asked Cousin Dorothy to purchase the Bible for me—but I didn't show how eager I was to read it. As soon as she left I opened to the beginning of the New Testament and began reading the Book of Matthew. It's hard to describe what I found so irresistible about Jesus. First of all, it was obvious that He was Jewish. The Book of Matthew begins with His genealogy and traces Him back as a son of David. That set my mind at ease because I saw from the start that I wasn't reading about some foreign religion."

While all four Gospels were written with some Jewish color, Matthew is the sole author who makes capital of it.

Links to opening and closing books of the Old Testament

Matthew's starting sentence, "The book of the generation of Jesus Christ" (1:1) is a conscious reference to Genesis, the first book in the Bible, where a similar expression occurs near its opening,

"This is the book of the generations of Adam" (5:1). Matthew links his writing to the beginning of the Old Testament.

Not only does Matthew go back to the early part of the Bible, but he also alludes to the last two verses in the Old Testament, involving a promise to "send you Elijah the prophet before the coming of the great and dreadful day of the Lord" (Mal. 4:4, 5). Without ruling out a future appearance of Elijah, Jesus declared that John the Baptist was that "Elias, which was to come" (Matt. 11:14). So Matthew goes back to where the Old Testament begins, and takes up where the Old Testament ends, relating to both Genesis and Malachi.

Links to two outstanding Old Testament personages

Matthew's opening verse says, "The book of the generation of Jesus Christ, the son of David, the son of Abraham" (1:1). This relates Jesus immediately to the two great covenants God made with these men. God's covenant to David included the promise of a king to sit upon His throne forever (2 Sam. 7:8-13).

God promised Abraham that through his offspring all nations of the earth would be blessed. Whereas David's son was to be a King, Abraham's son was to be sacrifice. Abraham's immediate son, Isaac, willingly offering himself on the altar in obedience to his father's command, typified the later Son Who would be obedient even unto death. Matthew's Gospel begins with the birth of a King, and ends with the offering of a sacrifice. Here is a short outline of Matthew, based on its opening verse.

I.	1:1–4:16	Introduction
II.	4:17–16:20	Jesus, as son of David, rejected as King
III.	16:21–28:20	Jesus, as son of Abraham, presented as sacrifice.

Links with Old Testament verses

I am now looking at a chart showing the use of the Old Testament by Matthew in the construction of his Gospel. This table lists 44 Old Testament quotations in one form or another. Also, it enumerates another 18 allusions, making a total of 62 references in Matthew to Israel's Scriptures. These overall figures vary little from scholar to scholar. Matthew has more Old Testament quotations than all other three Gospels combined.

Nineteen, over half of the Old Testament books, are cited by Matthew. The Holy Spirit led Matthew to choose all five books of the Pentateuch, three historical, two poetical, and nine prophetical, from which to obtain data for his account.

Fifteen characters are mentioned by Matthew: Abel, Noah, Abraham, Isaac, Jacob, Moses, David, Solomon, Queen of Sheba, Elijah, Isaiah, Jeremiah, Daniel, Jonah, and Zacharias, not including nearly 40 other names in the genealogy in chapter one.

Detailed handling, or even the bare listing of all these 62 references, is beyond the scope of this book. But their cumulative effect focuses on Jesus as the fulfiller of God's plan and of the prophet's predictions through the ages.

The following expressions, all directing back to the Old Testament, are characteristic of Matthew: "That it might be fulfilled", "It is written", "It was said by them of old time", and "Have ye not read?"

"That it might be fulfilled" and "It is written"

These two formulae appear about two dozen times in this Gospel. Though many Old Testament passages cited in Matthew derive from the Greek translation known as the Septuagint, "there is an interesting group of twelve passages (1:22*ff.*, 2:5*ff.*, 2:15, 2:17*ff.*, 2:23, 3:3, 4:14*ff.*, 8:17, 12:17-21, 13:35, 21:4*ff.*, 27:9) all of which, with the exception of 2:23 and 3:3 appear to be based to a greater or less degree on the Hebrew text. In each case they are preceded by the words, 'in order that that which was spoken by the prophets might be fulfilled', or words to that effect, and with a single exception (3:3) they are peculiar to Matthew's Gospel."[1]

"It was said by them of old time"

This sentence occurs six times (5:21, 27, 31, 33, 38, 43). Jesus, Who came not to destroy but to fulfill the law, cited six areas of conduct in which the scribes lacked full understanding: murder, adultery, divorce, oaths, retaliation, and love of neighbor. Jesus prefixed His instruction in each case with the above sentence, then amplified the Old Testament command to show its full spiritual interpretation. For example, the command against adultery cannot be limited to an overt act, but extends right into our thought life: lust is mental adultery.

---

1. Vincent Taylor, *The Gospels*, London: The Epworth Press, no date, p. 60.

"Have ye not read?"

Matthew links his Gospel with the Old Testament by assuming his hearers were familiar with the Scriptures. Seven times in His controversies with the Pharisees He rebuked their ignorance of the very volume which they supposedly knew so well. He referred to David eating the holy shewbread in the temple (12:3), priests in the temple profaning the sabbath (12:5); the creation of male and female (19:4), infants praising God (21:16), the rejection of the cornerstone (21:42), the resurrection of the dead (22:31), and Daniel's abomination of desolation (24:15). The question, "Have ye not read?" is found more in Matthew than in all other three Gospels combined.

Miscellaneous links

The only six specific *dreams* in the New Testament all occur in Matthew, all relating to the birth and infancy of Jesus, with the exception of the dream of Pilate's wife at Jesus' trial. Perhaps Matthew wished to remind his readers of the place dreams played in the lives of Old Testament heroes, Joseph and Daniel.

The flight into Egypt and return (2:13-15) would highlight a strong similarity with Israel's escape from Egyptian bondage.

Matthew is the only place in the New Testament where Jesus' country is called *"the land of Israel"* (2:20).

Jerusalem is called *"the holy city"* only in Matthew (4:5; 27:53).

In Jesus' controversy with the Pharisees over the disciples plucking grain on the Sabbath, Matthew, Mark, and Luke all report Jesus' reference to David eating shewbread on the Sabbath. But only Matthew adds Jesus' remarks about priests in the temple working on the Sabbath (Numbers 28:9, 10), and His comment, "in this place is One greater than the temple" (12:6). *The temple would be of interest to Jews, but of little concern to Gentiles.*

Matthew takes for granted that his readers were *familiar with Jewish customs* whereas Mark sometimes adds a little explanation (cf. Matt. 15:1, 2 and Mark 7:1-4; also Matt. 27:62 and Mark 15:42).

After Jesus healed multitudes, only in Matthew are we told that the people glorified the God *of Israel* (15:31).

Pertinent mainly to Jews is Jesus' warning, only in Matthew, that the "kingdom of God shall be taken from you, and given to a nation bringing forth the fruits thereof" (21:43).

While all four evangelists quote Old Testament prophecies fulfilled in the sufferings and death of Christ, Matthew gives details omitted by the others. He describes at least nineteen *events closely paralleling prophetic predictions.* For example, whereas Mark and Luke simply say that Jesus was betrayed for money, which John does not mention, Matthew gives the specific price of thirty pieces of silver (26:15), as foretold by Zechariah (11:12). Also, though all gospels record Joseph of Arimathaea's burial of Jesus in his own tomb, only Matthew tells us that Joseph was rich (27:57), a reference to Isaiah (53:9).

Two witnesses

More than once, Matthew declares that two people were healed, while both Mark and Luke mention just one. For example, in Matthew (8:28-34) two Gadarenes are healed of demons. But Mark (5:1-21) and Luke (8:26-40) tell of one healed. Similarly, Matthew (9:27-31) reports Jesus giving sight to two blind men. But Mark (10:46-52) and Luke (18:35-43) speak of one.

The critics claim contradiction, but the accounts are likely complementary. Two were given sight, but Mark and Luke were interested more in one particular blind beggar, named Bartimaeus. Had either Mark or Luke specifically stated that only one had been healed, we would have a problem. A baseball fan, reporting on an exciting game, emphasized a game-winning home run hit by the team's star slugger in the ninth inning, when in reality, the star hit two home runs in the same game. But the earlier homer was overshadowed by the later crucial blow.

Why does Matthew relate the healing of two demoniacs and of two blind men? The Old Testament required a minimum of two witnesses to attest to an event. "One witness shall not rise up against a man for any iniquity, . . . at the mouth of two witnesses or at the mouth of three witnesses, shall the matter be established" (Deut. 19:15). Since writing to people familiar with this Old Testament law, Matthew mentions double healings: two witnesses attest to the power of Christ.

Matthew's penchant for "two" also occurs in his account of the triumphal entry, where he mentions two animals, the donkey and its colt (21:2, 7). The other Gospels mention only the colt. Matthew points out that this incident fulfills Zechariah 9:9 where two animals are mentioned, another evidence of his emphasis on the fulfillment of Old Testament prophecy.

Kingdom of heaven

The phrase, "kingdom of heaven" occurs about 32 times, only in Matthew, but is used interchangeably with "kingdom of God" in other Gospels. When Matthew reports Jesus saying of little children, "of such is the kingdom of heaven" (19:14), Mark (10:14) and Luke (18:16) have it, "of such is the kingdom of God." Also, in Jesus' warning in Matthew of the difficulty rich people have in entering "the kingdom of heaven" (19:23), Mark (10:23) and Luke (18:24) refer to "the kingdom of God."

Some scholars find a dispensational distinction between the kingdom of heaven and the kingdom of God. Another reason for its appearance in Matthew may be a concession to Jewish reluctance to pronounce the word "God." In their oaths Jews would swear by the earth, by Jerusalem, by the temple, or by heaven, to avoid speaking the name of God. The repeated use of "kingdom of heaven" as a substitute for "kingdom of God" may provide additional evidence of the Jewishness of this Gospel.

Summing up, a strong feature of Matthew is belief that Jesus' life and death is the consummation of the Old Testament writings. Matthew's strategy to reach his kinsfolk by appealing to fulfilled prophecy has its present-day proponents. In 1982 Jews for Jesus launched a campaign to reach fellow-Jews through the secular print media, using a full-page ad with a large printed announcement, "The Messiah Has Come and His Name is Y'shua." The ad explained how Y'shua was the Jewish way to say Jesus, listed prophecies from the Old Testament which pointed to Him, and invited inquirers to send for a free book, titled *Y'shua*, containing an exposition of Old Testament Messianic prophecies. With believers shouldering the expense, 90 newspapers, including the *New York Times*, published this statement. Over 100,000 responded to the ad, many of whom professed to accept Jesus as their Messiah.

TOPICAL

As a tax-collector, Matthew had a thing for numbers and orderly arrangement. When he heard Jesus say, "Follow me," he closed his ledger, dropped his quill, stumbled out from behind his desk, and shut his booth, but he was not finished with his bookkeeping. Jesus saw great potential in this disciplined, keen, good-with-figures, despised publican, transformed his life, and inspired Him to write the first book in the New Testament.

This accountant was the ideal choice to trace Jesus' genealogy through the royal line to David and then to Abraham. Matthew's love of numbers shows up in his grouping of three sets of fourteen in his construction of the genealogy.

But where his interest for systemization appears most evident is in his topical arrangements. Though Matthew covers much the same territory as the other Gospels, chronological sequence is not the main concern of his writing. He seems to have brought together most of Jesus' teachings on various subjects in concentrated sections. His account is more topical than sequential. He builds his Gospel around five main discourses, closing each one with a similar statement, "And it came to pass that when Jesus had finished these sayings" or "parables" or "had made an end of commanding."

- the Sermon on the Mount - - - - - - - - 5:1 – 7:28
- instructions to the Twelve - - - - - - - - 10:1 – 11:1
- seven parables of the kingdom - - - - - - 13:1 – 13:53
  (half of the 14 parables in this Gospel)
- lifestyles in the kingdom - - - - - - - - 18:1 – 19:1
  (including humility and forgiveness)
- Olivet discourse - - - - - - - - - - - - 24:1 – 26:1

Three of the sections include the first verse of the following chapter, which those responsible for chapter divisions probably should have included with the previous chapter.

Other topical groupings include chapters 8 and 9, which are devoted to accounts of ten miracles, half of the twenty miracles found in all of this Gospel, and chapter 23 which rocks with Jesus' repeated woes pronounced on the hypocritical leaders for misleading the people. Matthew, whose pen had once been given over to making notations in a questionable trade, became dedicated to copying notes on Jesus' discourses and miracles, and to presenting them in logical and systematic fashion.

KINGLY

In this Gospel the word "king" is applied to the Lord Jesus 14 times. "Kingdom" is found 17 times; the phrase, "kingdom of heaven," 32 times; and "kingdom of God," 5 times. In all, these "royalty" words are found 68 times.

Son of David

Matthew, who stresses Jesus' kingship, traces his stock through David, renowned monarch of Israel. The first phrase in the first verse is "Jesus, the son of David" (1:1). Then five verses later David is called "the king" twice in the same sentence (1:6). "Son of David" was a kingly title, linking the promised heir to the promised throne. Jesus is called "son of David" eight times in Matthew, a title rarely used in the other Gospels (1:1; 9:27; 12:23; 15:22; 20:30, 31; 21:9, 15).

Matthew uses the title in stories in which other Gospel authors omit it. For example, according to Matthew the Canaanitish woman, pleading for her ill daughter, addresses Him, "Thou Son of David" (15:22). But Mark omits this title (7:24-30). Similarly, at the healing of a demon-possessed, blind mute Matthew reports the reaction of the crowd, "Is not this the son of David?" (12:23). Luke, however, mentions the wonder of the people but omits the appellation (11:14).

The Wise Men

Only Matthew records the visit of the eastern Magi who asked, "Where is He that is born King of the Jews?" (2:2). They brought gifts befitting royalty (2:11). The other Gospels, not emphasizing His kingly role, omit this story. Only Matthew mentions rival king Herod (2:1-23).

Forerunner

John the Baptist heralds the Savior's imminent appearance in all four Gospels, but only Matthew has the forerunner speaking in terms of the kingdom (3:1, 2).

Temptation

Matthew and Luke relate the story of Jesus' temptation. Though both begin with the stones-into-bread test, they reverse the second and third enticements, so that Matthew's final test deals with Satan's offer of all the kingdoms of this world in return for Jesus' worship. It's not surprising that Matthew, who stresses the Kingship of Christ, makes the kingdom appeal climactic (4:1-11). In a later chapter we'll see why Luke makes the pinnacle-jumping inducement the final test (4:1-13).

Sermon on the Mount

This discourse serves as the King's inaugural address, outlining the basic standards of His coming realm.

Luke's shorter version of the Sermon on the Mount places Jesus on a plain, after descending from a higher level (6:17). To deliver this message, Matthew positions Jesus sitting on a mountain, an elevated spot more suited to a King (5:1).

The Lord's Prayer

What is commonly called "The Lord's Prayer" ends abruptly in Luke, omitting the triumphant climax of Matthew's version with its kingdom emphasis, "For thine is the kingdom, and the power, and the glory, for ever. Amen" (6:13; Luke 11:2-4).

But I Say Unto You

Someone counted over 50 times Jesus used this imperious expression, "But I say unto you," which so often placed His own utterances on the same level as the words from Mount Sinai, not only correcting earlier prophets but even superseding them. How irritating these words must have sounded in the ears of His opponents who so heatedly disputed His claim to Messiahship. But these words indeed ring with the authority of the King.

Parables of the Kingdom

The seven parables of chapter 13 deal with the kingdom.

Temple Tax

Only Matthew records Jesus paying the temple tax (17:24-27). Jesus implied that as a King He was exempt from payment, but to avoid needless offense, He told Peter to pay the tax with a coin lodged in the mouth of the first fish he caught. This incident, related to the temple, had more relevance to Jewish readers.

Introduction to Parables

Matthew and Luke include similar (though varying) parables about invitations to feasts. But the difference in the opening sentences fits the purpose of each writer. Matthew has "a certain king, which made a marriage for his son" (22:2). But Luke, who presents Jesus as man, begins, "A certain man made a great supper, and bade many" (14:16). In Matthew's record the king casts out those not wearing a wedding garment (22:13).

The Sheep and the Goats

The judgment at the Second Coming, separating sheep from goats, is peculiar to Matthew. The Son of Man is portrayed on the royal throne of His glory, judging the nations. Comes the verdict, "Then shall the King say unto them on His right hand, Come, ye blessed of my Father" (25:34). When asked the reason for the reward, we read that "the King shall answer" (25:40).

Majesty at His Passion

At Jesus' arrest in Gethsemane, Peter drew his sword and cut off the ear of the high priest's servant. Only Matthew records Jesus' rebuke to Peter, "Thinkest thou that I cannot now pray to my Father, and He shall presently give me more than twelve legions of angels?" (26:53). Jesus was saying, in effect, "I, as King, command an invisible army. The mere beckon of my finger would immediately summon armies of angels." Matthew frequently refers to "His angels" (e.g., 13:41; 16:27; 24:31). In giving the Great Commission only Matthew includes the preface, "All power is given unto Me in heaven and in earth" (28:18).

Worship

The verb "worship" is composed of two words, "before" and "kiss," meaning to fall before someone and kiss his hand in reverence. Kings received such homage from their subjects. Often in Matthew, rarely in the other Gospels, people worshiped Jesus (2:2, 8, 11; 8:2; 9:18; 14:33; 15:25; 20:20; 28:9, 17).

The Kingdom—Present and Future

The King was rejected by His people. Matthew gave a strong hint of Gentile welcome into the kingdom when He warned that the children of the kingdom would be cast out, and "That many shall come from the east and west, and shall sit down with Abraham, Isaac, and Jacob, in the kingdom of heaven" (8:11, 12). Only Matthew mentions the church by name (16:18; 18:17): the mystery of Jew and Gentile united in one body.

The kingdom has a dual aspect: present and future. In the present the kingdom pertains to the spiritual realm where Jesus has rule over the hearts of people. Jesus said, "The kingdom of God is within you" (Luke 17:21), and "My kingdom is not of this world" (John 18:36). Entrance comes through the new birth. As Jesus said, "Except a man be born again, he cannot see the kingdom of God" (John 3:3). Saved initially from the guilt of sin, believers than are saved progressively from the dominion of evil, as the kingdom of God has growing sway in their lives.

The future aspect of the kingdom refers to that day when Jesus will return and establish His rule on earth. When He appears, believers will be like Him, fashioned completely in His image, their salvation culminated. Then it will be said, "The kingdoms of this world are become the kingdoms of our Lord, and of His Christ; and He shall reign forever and ever" (Rev. 11:15). Then He will govern our world with righteousness that shall cover the earth, as the waters cover the sea.

Charles R. Eerdman wrote of that glorious day in the Foreword to his commentary on *The Gospel of Matthew* several decades ago, "The hopes of this world are to be realized in the reign of an unusual king. The seething unrest of nations, the savageries of war, the threatenings of anarchy increase the yearning for the rule of One Whose wisdom is faultless, whose love is perfect, whose power is supreme. Such a ruler is Christ under Whose scepter the earth is to attain its age of glory." [2] If such conditions were true in 1920, how much more eagerly today do we pray, "Thy kingdom come."

In the next chapter we think of the present significance of Jesus' kingdom. We ask ourselves, "Is He the King of my life?"

---

2. Westminster Press, 1920.

4

Who Is the King of Your Life?

D r. Nick Georghita, Romanian endocrinologist who spent three months in training at the Mayo Clinic, gave up his medical career of twenty-five years in 1981 to become pastor of the Second Baptist Church in Oradea, Romania. His decision infuriated Romania's communist authorities who tried unsuccessfully to persuade this well-known doctor to withdraw from the pastorate and return to his practice. For several years he was harassed by the secret police, and had to move frequently. Because he spoke out boldly against the communist regime, his life was frequently threatened.

A group of pastors, meeting in October 1989, discussed what topics they would preach on at Christmas time. They decided to emphasize the following truths: Jesus is on the throne yesterday, today and forever; other kingdoms will be changed, but not Jesus' kingdom; His kingdom is unshakable. They knew that preaching these messages would have its cost.

A week before Christmas the local communist council came to

Georghita with an order. "This Christmas you are not allowed to go into the streets and sing Christmas carols this year. This is a command from Bucharest and the leadership of the party." Georghita replied, "We will do it."

When Christmas Eve came, it was impossible to sing Christmas carols in the streets. The masses had revolted against the government. The dictator had been caught trying to escape and was shot. The picture of his slain body was shown on TV. The streets were full of soldiers and cheering crowds.

But on the second day after Christmas the people congregated in the main square of Oradea, in front of the communist headquarters, and began to shout, "We want to listen to the pastor of the Second Baptist Church." They sent for Georghita. He brought his choir. They sang Christmas carols. He preached. Then he said, "We want to pray. We don't know if you know the Lord's Prayer. Would you be so kind as to bow your head and say it after us." Despite forty years of antichristian propaganda, thousands knelt in the street and recited the Lord's Prayer.

The new president of Romania now permits churches to meet freely, distribute Bibles, evangelize openly, and start schools, clinics, and orphanages. Georghita helped organize the Evangelical Alliance of Romania, was elected Secretary General of the Romanian Baptist church, and was awarded the prize for religious freedom by the Institute for Religion and Democracy.

The unshakable kingdom of Jesus, which these Romanian pastors declared that Christmas time, has a dual significance. In one sense His kingdom is yet future, awaiting His return to earth to establish universal peace and righteousness (2 Tim. 4:1). In another sense the kingdom is present within us here and now. Jesus spoke of receiving the kingdom as a little child (Mk. 10:15), and of seeking first "His kingdom and His righteousness" (Matt. 6:23). To enjoy His future kingdom we must yield to His sway in our hearts in this life. To pray "Thy kingdom come," is to ask not only for His yet future Second Coming, but also for His will to be "done in earth, as it is in heaven."

Claiming all authority, Jesus commissioned His followers to proclaim His kingdom to every nation. This soon brought them into direct confrontation with the Roman kingdom. When His followers refused to worship the emperor, Roman authorities who acknowledged "no king but Caesar" accused Christians of "saying that there is another king, one called Jesus" (Acts 17:7 NIV). Those who declined to offer incense before the emperor's statue were often tortured, jailed, or fed to the lions.

Through the centuries Christian conscience has repeatedly found itself in battle with political mandates or societal values. In asserting his loyalty to Jesus Christ, a seventeenth-century Covenanter said to King James VI of Scotland, "There are two kings and two kingdoms in Scotland. There is King James, the head of the Commonwealth, and there is Jesus Christ, the King of the church."

During World War II, when Korea was under the control of the Japanese military, the five thousand members of forty small Korean churches met faithfully for worship. The Japanese commanders called in the Baptist association's chief pastor for interrogation. After hours of exhausting questioning, the military authorities asked, "What do you believe about the second coming?" When the pastor replied, "We believe that this same Jesus shall so return as He went away," the Japanese military continued, "And then what?"

"And then," said the pastor, "every knee shall bow and every tongue confess that He is Lord to the glory of God the Father."

"Does that include our divine emperor?" asked the military.

The pastor responded, "Sir, it includes your emperor, for our Savior is the King of kings and the Lord of lords."

The commander then queried, "Do you believe this for yourself alone, or do all of you believe it?"

The pastor answered, "Sir, we all believe it."

The military rounded up and imprisoned all forty of their pastors. After four years of incarceration and persecution, the chief pastor died of exposure. One by one, most of the other pastors also died. When finally the few who survived were liberated, two of them died soon after. These pastors paid a great price for their loyalty to Jesus' kingdom here on earth! They will doubtless be honored in His kingdom yet future.

Not surprisingly, Chuck Colson titled a book, *Kingdoms in Conflict.* Several colleges indicate by name or motto where their loyalties lie, like *The King's College*, near New York City. *Wheaton College*, just west of Chicago, has the motto, "For Christ and His Kingdom." Every segment of a believer's life should come under submission to his or her King.

TIME

The only mention of Matthew's name in his Gospel is the incident of his call to follow Jesus (9:9). Leaving all, ledger, quill, booth and business, he responded immediately, an action befitting his emphasis on the kingship of Jesus. Matthew also records the instantaneous obedience of Peter, Andrew, James, and John to a similar call. From the moment of their summons, the time of all these disciples belonged completely to their Master. Though most of us are not called into what is called full-time service, we are nevertheless full-time subjects.

Each of us has the same amount of time, sixty seconds to the minute, sixty minutes to the hour, and twenty-four hours to the day. The President of the USA has no more time to do his mammoth job than any of us; granted he has more help. Some day we must answer for this marvelous gift of time. Asked what they are doing, some respond, "I've been killing time." What did time ever do to us that we should murder it? We are to *redeem* time.

We should devote time to worship. On a missionary trip to Africa in 1986 I spoke in a Sunday morning service in Zaire. My thirty-minute message, translated into two dialects, consumed an hour-and-a-half altogether. The service with songs, prayers and testimonies lasted three hours. The crowd of three hundred, clogging every window and doorway in the small frame church, patiently participated. I recall wondering how the average American congregation would react to such a lengthy service.

We should schedule time for study and meditation in God's Word. A Monday night football addict faced a hard decision when his church announced a fall, twelve-week Monday evening Bible course. He rationalized that, since Monday was always a hard day at work, he deserved the relaxation of watching the game. But reminding himself that his time belonged to the Lord, he attended the class, and found himself home in time for most of the game.

Time in Bible memorization is well spent. A ministerial student determined to memorize Scripture to help in his witnessing. He began by memorizing one verse every morning while shaving, learning the reference as well. Each day he would review several earlier verses which, when mastered thoroughly, required less frequent review. Some years later he had memorized 20,000 of the approximately 31,000 verses in the Bible, and was not only able to recite them accurately, but also to cite their exact location in book, chapter, and verse. When I was fifteen, he came to our church for an evangelistic crusade. His sermons, saturated with Bible quotes, brought conviction and salvation to my life. I am glad that he gave time to Scripture memorization.

We should give time to service. Some have established music libraries for the church choir, prepared advertising copy, tutored the underprivileged, driven the elderly to medical appointments, repaired church property, led small groups, or contacted prospects. Some doctors, nurses, teachers, and builders have gone out as short-term missionaries for six months.

Someone estimated that in a lifetime of seventy years we spend three years in education, eight at the dinner table, five in transportation, four in conversation, fourteen in work, three in reading, twenty in sleeping, three in convalescing, nine in watching TV, and far less than one year in spiritual activity if we go to a ninety-minute church service Sunday mornings and spend several minutes in prayer daily.

How do you spend your time as a Christian? Kingdom priorities may require saying no to excess partying, long phone conversations, aimless shopping, trashy books, or banal TV.

MONEY

In a two-part cartoon the first scene pictured the grave of Jim Elliot, a missionary martyred by the Aucas, with his familiar quote, "He is no fool who gives what he cannot keep to gain what he cannot lose." In the second section was the drawing of a spacious home with swimming pool, two late-model cars, a large yard with outdoor equipment, two TV sets, elaborate furniture, and in a lounge chair on the patio a young yuppie, by his side his wife who had just handed him a letter. Together they exclaim, "Another missionary appeal! We gave our tithe. Surely no one expects us to give more!"

We do not discharge our obligation to God by giving our tithe; all ten tenths belong to Him. The other nine tenths constitute an expense account given us by our King. Just as an employee would find it impossible to justify the purchase from his expense account of a fur coat for his wife or a motorcycle for his son, so many Christians will suffer remorse at the King's final audit for purchasing unjustifiable items.

In biblical times a steward was the administrator of his master's estate, managing domestic concerns, handling servants, collecting rents or income, and keeping accounts. Eleazar, Abraham's steward, ran Abraham's affairs, even taking his master's jewels on a trip to find a bride for Abraham's son. But steward Eleazar didn't own Abraham's house, money, servants, or jewels. He only supervised them.

Jesus never condemned the rich for having riches, but for acting as if the riches were theirs. It's not wrong to be rich, but to be a rich fool. A fool, whether rich or poor, is one who considers his possessions his own, inwardly saying, "My barns, my fruits, my goods." Not ownership, but stewardship, is kingdom teaching. Strangely, when we give money to the King, we only give Him what really belongs to Him.

World Vision magazine (December 1988 - January 1989) carried a fascinating article, "The Profit Prophet," which related the stewardship philosophy of financier Gary Ginter. In his thirty-third floor office in downtown Chicago, as one of four founding partners, he helps direct Chicago Research and Trading Group Ltd., a multi-million-dollar futures and options trading firm, mentioned favorably in the *Wall Street Journal*. Yet his lifestyle has been likened more to Sears than to Saks.

After ten years of business flops, he founded CRT in 1977 and saw a rapid ballooning of $150,000 base capital into a total above $250 million in the next eleven years. He shuttles between Chicago and an office in Washington, D.C., and often to Tokyo. CRT enables him to give substantially to foreign missions. About 80% of the firm's giving is invested in missionary corporations and kingdom companies.

"A kingdom company," he explains, "is organized to achieve kingdom goals as opposed to financial goals. That doesn't mean it's not designed to break even in the long term. It's designed to do exactly that. But its motivation is not to maximize return on investment measured by dollars, but rather to maximize return on investment measured by kingdom standards. A missionary corporation is simply a kingdom company that operates in a cross-cultural setting, whether that be inner city to suburban, rich to poor, white to black, or Africa to America. . . ." (p. 21). Among the more successful kingdom companies is World Craftsmen, which imports and distributes hand-tied fishing flies from Kenya and Guatemala, and also provides work for 140 Third World people. Recently World Craftsmen ranked among the top four fishing fly wholesalers in North America.

Also, Ginter's Jubilee Foundation underwrote the entire marketing cost for the U.S. Center for World Mission's "Last $1,000" campaign, which resulted in the successful retirement of an $8 million debt on the center's campus center, home to more than forty missionary research and sending organizations.

Says Ginter, "God has called me to make all the money I can, but live on as little as possible, and give the rest away," an accurate way of expressing the kingship of Jesus in money matters. Matthew reported Jesus' command to lay up treasure in heaven, rather than on earth (6:19-21). Obedience down here now will provide dividends in the kingdom up there later.

ABILITIES

A magazine ad read, "If you like to draw, you may have a God-given talent. I can't think of a greater waste than being blessed with a natural ability and doing nothing about it."

To fail to deploy our abilities is not only a waste but a sin according to a parable recorded by Matthew. A master, going on a long trip, gave five talents to one servant, two to another, and one to a third servant. On his return the master called for an accounting. The servants with five and two talents each doubled the master's investment, earning his approval. But the one with the lone talent buried it, receiving a scathing rebuke. The energy expended burying it should have been spent on walking to the moneychangers where it would have earned interest (25:14-30).

Why do some people have musical ability, others linguistic aptitude, and others mathematical proficiency? Why do some have many talents, and others few? The talents were distributed according to the sovereign pleasure of the Master—as He willed. God does not give talents or spiritual gifts to each one equally. Each one received at least one talent, suggesting that no one can say, "I don't have any ability whatsoever." But whatever talents He does assign us are to be used for the promotion of His kingdom. To whom more is given, much is required.

A danger lurks for those possessing several talents. Because learning comes easily, the gifted student is tempted to slide along, seldom opening a book. His A grade may not be as high in the King's estimation as the A mark of the B-average student, who has to work harder to equal the gifted's A grade.

Danger also threatens the one-talented. "My talent won't be missed," he thinks, so neglects to use it. But the King needs small talents too. A small man said to a large man, "If I were as big as you, I would go into the woods, find me a big bear, and pull that big bear limb from limb." The big man retorted, "There are some little bears in the woods too. Let's see what you can do." Failure to use a talent is not only disobedience to the King, but also a waste of His resources, even robbery. Many or few, we should use whatever talents God has given us.

To use a talent with slipshod diligence is a slap at the King Who wishes a good return on His investment. The prophet Malachi rebuked the priests for offering blemished sacrifices (1:8). They brought to their heavenly God what they would not dare present to their earthly governor. A Sunday school teacher asked herself, "If I knew that next week Billy Graham would sit in on my class and observe the way I teach, would I spend more time in preparation and try to do a better job?" We should never forget that the Lord sits in on our class every Sunday, and observes the degree of faithfulness in the use of our abilities.

I have attended and enjoyed many public audience radio broadcasts and TV telecasts through the years. I have never failed to come away without admiring the professionalism of those involved. The programs ran like clockwork, starting at the precise moment, following a deftly crafted script, with flawless performance and super music, and ending on the dot. And they did this for money, prestige, fulfillment, and career advancement. Almost every time I had this thought, "How different from many church services which start late, and stumble along in an inferior, careless manner. And we are supposedly giving our best to the Master." Jesus said that "the children of this world are considerably more shrewd in dealing with their contemporaries than the children of light" (Luke 16:8, Phillps). The King's work demands the best use of abilities in all of life: job, school, home, community, and church. Faithfulness on our part will merit His "Well done."

SPEECH

Jesus, whose reign extends to the tongue, warned that every thoughtless word would some day be judged (Matt. 12:36). Malicious gossip, boasting, falsehood, suggestiveness, slander, unkind criticism, murmuring, and profanity are off limits to the King's subjects. Though the tongue is a little body member, and so unruly, the degree to which a person controls his speech reflects his level of spirituality and submission to his Master.

A word spoken at a fitting moment is like apples of gold in a frame of silver. The tongue can be so happily used for praise, prayer, teaching, and encouragement. Would a word of uplift have made a difference in the life of John Dillinger, notorious gangster in the 1930s who was gunned down on a Chicago street by the FBI? An author relates an incident from Rex Humbard's *Answer* magazine. After a service in the Cadle Tabernacle in 1942, a lady shook Humbard's hand and said, "Rex, you don't know me, but I want to thank you for praying with those young people. Years ago my brother got into trouble in our community. People there told their children, 'Don't have anything to do with John, because he's a bad boy.' We had a meeting in a country church and one night during the meeting John's heart was moved. He got up out of his seat and came down the altar. But because no one came to pray with him, in just a few moments John got up and walked to the back of the church. He looked at me and said, 'I'm never going into another church again.' He didn't. My brother's name was John Dillinger." Tears welled up in that woman's eyes as she told her story."[1]

We easily talk about the weather, the stock market, current events, and sports, but sometimes find it difficult to speak a word for our King Who has asked us to confess Him before men. We would not want Him ashamed of us in heaven because we were ashamed to own His name on earth.

Major league baseball player Jose Alou recounts in *Decision* magazine how when playing shortstop for the San Francisco Giants in a 1962 World Series game, New York Yankee Bobby Richardson slammed a double and landed on second base. Playing close to second, Jose heard Bobby call, "Jose!" Jose thought, "What would the Yankee second baseman want with me in the middle of a World Series game? I knew he was a Christian. Reason must be to confuse me." Bobby called again, "Jose, I want to know—do you know the Lord?" Jose, who had taken a stand for Christ shortly before the World Series, nodded "Yes." Jose could never forget the sight of Bobby Richardson's face and the sound of his voice, a star player

---

1. R. Alan Street, *The Effective Invitation*, Revell, 1984, pp. 181, 182.

right in the middle of baseball's most exciting series, speaking for Christ. Jose became a bolder witness.

ETHICAL PRINCIPLES

Former University of Michigan College football coach Bo Schembechler remembers as a boy a phone call which greatly angered his father. His father's rival for the position of fire chief had somehow gotten hold of the civil service exam. His father was a fire captain, qualified, and wanted the job badly. But candidates had to take the exam, and somehow his opponent now had a copy of the questions. The phone call was from his pals at the club who somehow also had secured a copy, and were offering him a chance to cheat before he was cheated on. "It's only fair," they urged. But his father refused to look at the questions in advance. He took the test cleanly, scored very high, but his rival beat him by a point, and was made fire chief. His father walked up to his rival, looked him squarely in the eye, and said, "I know how you got that score. And I am not working for you." He took a lesser position, became a fire inspector, and died doing that job. But son Bo said that he learned more from that incident than any other lesson from childhood. It taught him not to bend his principles, even if it cost and "everybody else is doing it."

The King outlined the moral principles of His kingdom in the Sermon on the Mount: meekness, purity, sanctity of life, honesty, genuine worship, kindness in judging others, truthfulness, contentment, and love of enemies, among other qualities. He wants us to maintain our convictions in all these areas.

Who hasn't been inspired by the example of Eric Liddell, whose life was dramatized in the movie, *Chariots of Fire?* Born of Scottish missionary parents in China, schooled in Scotland and excelling in track, he was chosen to represent Great Britain in the 1924 Olympic games in Paris. Learning that the 100-meter heats were scheduled on Sunday, he refused to run. Criticism and jibes couldn't move him. Withdrawing from the 100-meter, he was given a spot in the 400. Though not trained for this event, he won the hearts of the British people by both winning a gold medal and establishing a new world's record. A year later he returned to China as a missionary. After a twenty-year ministry, he died in a Japanese internment camp. He was a man of conviction. Even an attempt by the Prince of Wales to urge him to run the Sunday race failed—Eric Liddell served higher royalty.

When Buzz Aldrin landed on the moon in July 1969, he was determined to give thanks to God for a safe landing. But how to go about fulfilling his conviction? He had been forbidden to do so because of the many complaints when a former Apollo crew had read over the air passages from Genesis the previous Christmas Eve while orbiting the moon. NASA wanted no more confrontations from antireligious groups. Aldrin requested a short moment of silence. With microphone off, he opened a little Communion kit prepared by his Presbyterian pastor, and poured wine from a vial the size of the tip of his finger into a tiny cup. In the moon's light gravity the liquid swirled around the miniature cup. Before going back on the air, he ate a little piece of bread, swallowed the wine, and silently gave thanks for the safe trip to the moon's Sea of Tranquillity. He was acknowledging his King.[2]

FULL ALLEGIANCE

Some years ago the editors of a leading London newspaper were chagrined to find several typographical errors in their editions every day. Someone hit upon an idea. The typesetters were told that the first issue of each day's paper would be delivered to the king of England. Suddenly the paper became virtually free of errors, as they realized that a their work came under the scrutiny of His Majesty.

Our King deserves the kind of allegiance which governed the life of missionary David Livingstone. When Hollywood was filming *With Stanley in Africa*, the director said, "It's not hard to build scenes of jungle life and create the atmosphere of Africa, but how can we get across to the public the power that sent David Livingstone out to Africa and kept him there through all his unbelievable trials right to the very end?" The answer is found in Livingstone's diary. He had penned this entry on his second-to-last birthday, "My Jesus, my King, my Life, my All, I again dedicate my whole self to Thee."

---

2. *New York Times,* July 2, 1989, Book Review Section, review by Fred Howard of *Men from Earth* by Buzz Aldrin and Malcolm McConnell, Bantam Books.

5

Specially in Mark

At the World's Fair in Brussels some years ago the Belgian Gospel Mission reported many unusual conversations with inquiring visitors at their Bible Pavilion. One of the mission's Russian-speaking workers, dining at a nearby restaurant, came in contact with several Russians employed at the Soviet Pavilion, and succeeded in luring some of them to their Bible display on the promise of finding books in their own language. Surveying the various portions of the Scriptures, one of the Russians suddenly shouted delight at finding a Gospel in Russian. Every one in the group took a book, expressing thanks for the copy of the "Gospel of Marx." The worker commented, "We hope they read the book even after discovering their mistake."

Marx and Mark have something in common—the theme of work. Some of Marx's followers consider him the patron saint of the worker; Mark presents Jesus as the Ideal Worker. Whereas Matthew portrays Him as mighty King; Mark paints Him as lowly Servant.

Though in early centuries commentaries were penned on the other Gospels, scholars gave little attention to Mark, judging it an abbreviation of Matthew and Luke. Yet five percent of Mark's material is not found in Matthew or Luke, giving the second Gospel a flavor all its own. Authentic touches add color to familiar scenes, enhancing the author's sketch of Jesus as Servant.

A bird's-eye outline, based on the Gospel's key verse (10:45), emphasizes that Jesus came to earth both as Servant and Savior. Nearly half of the book deals with His final week.

I.   *The Servant Came*
     1: 1-13— "For even the Son of Man came"

II. *The Servant Ministered*
     1:14 - 9:50— "not to be ministered unto, but to minister,"

III. *The Servant Gave His Life a Ransom*
     10: 1 - 16:20— "and to give His life a ransom for many."

Three words characterize Mark's Gospel: *Roman, busyness,* and *servanthood.*

ROMAN

Several little clues point to the Romans as the target of this Gospel. The author is John Mark. John was his Jewish name; Mark, his Roman. The Gospel goes by his Roman surname. Because the Romans had little interest in the Jewish Scriptures, Mark rarely quotes from the Old Testament, this in contrast to Matthew, who in writing to the Jews quoted the Scriptures on almost every page. Mark explains Aramaic words not understood by Roman readers like *Boanerges* (3:17) and *Talitha cumi* (5:41).

The Romans—a people of action

Mark appeals to the Romans, a nation of exploits, by picturing Jesus as a doer, a man of action. Brevity and vividness characterize his style. Shortest of the Gospels, the narrative seems to run. If the other Gospels seem a series of slides, Mark's is a movie. Other Gospels have long introductions, but Mark takes only 20 short verses to describe the ministry of John the Baptist, Jesus' baptism, His temptation in the wilderness, and the call of Peter, Andrew, James, and John (1:1-20). After this short introduction, Jesus starts serving.

With a picturesqueness of detail that frequently excels the other Gospels, Mark moves with breathtaking rapidity from scene to scene, house to house, synagogue to synagogue, and from town to town.

People and places keep changing. It's hard to keep up with him. A leper needs healing. A paralytic needs the use of his limbs. A demoniac needs release from possession.

The style is terse, free-flowing, and often discontinuous. Less didactic than the other Gospels, Mark depends for effect on the pungency of his description, which, says Merrill C. Tenney, "is intended to catch public attention in much the same way that a street preacher will hold an audience by the use of illustrations."[1] Matthew and Luke report that at Jesus' baptism the heavens were opened to Him; Mark says that Jesus saw the heavens rent open (1:10). In Gethsemane Matthew says that Jesus began to be sorrowful; Mark uses a stronger term, to be sore amazed (14:33).

Vividness is accentuated by repetition, a form of energy common in the Latin language. For example, the healed leper "began to publish it much, and to blaze abroad the matter" (1:45). The good seed "sprang up and increased" (4:8). Those who saw Jairus' daughter after Jesus raised her from the dead, "were astonished with a great astonishment" (5:42). Peter, denying his Lord in the high priest's quarters, says, "I know not, neither understand I what thou sayest" (14:68).

Mark does not write his Gospel in as chronological a sequence as Luke. Nor does He divide it into topical segments as Matthew. Nor does he depend on discourses as John, but gives us episode after episode, each painting an individual impression of Jesus. Tenney says that Mark does not rely on logical succession or extended argument but upon cumulative effect and pictorial appeal for his interpretation of Jesus.[2] So, he lets the story tell itself, and at least 23 times notes how men reacted to Jesus' deeds and words (1:27; 2:7, 12, 16; 3:6, 11, 21, 22; 4:41; 5:20, 42; 6:2, 14, 51; 7:37; 8:27-29; 10:24, 26, 32; 11:18; 12:12, 17, 34). People marveled, or were amazed, or feared exceedingly, or were astonished, or glorified God. People agreed that Jesus was an extraordinary person.

The Romans would appreciate the influence of Peter on the Gospel

Earliest and unbroken tradition regards the Gospel of Mark as containing, in essence, the story of Jesus as told by Peter. We could almost say the four Gospels are: Matthew, Peter, Luke and John.

---

1. *The Genius of the Gospels*, Eerdmans, 1951, p. 54.
2. *Ibid.*, p. 81.

Mark's mother, Mary, opened her spacious home in Jerusalem as a meeting place for the disciples, likely the site of the Upper Room. Here many times young Mark heard Peter relate with gusto Jesus' miracles and teachings. To Mary's home Peter gravitated on his sudden release from prison the night before his scheduled execution (Acts 12:12). Peter speaks of Mark as his son, suggesting that he led the youth to trust in Christ. When Mark was with Peter in Rome, he would have had ample opportunity to write down Peter's vivid firsthand accounts of Jesus' exploits (1 Pet. 5:13). Tradition says that Mark published his Gospel at Rome after Peter's death.

Mark frequently gives a more detailed report of certain episodes than found elsewhere. The raising of Jairus' daughter (5:21-43), the cleansing of the Gadarene demoniac (5:1-20), and the healing of the demon-possessed boy (9:14-29), all seem to indicate an eyewitness account. Here are a few examples that show the influence of Peter. Mark, not present, must have learned these facts from the ebullient leader of the Twelve.

- that Jesus was asleep on a pillow in a storm (4:38)
- that about 2,000 swine ran into the lake (5:13)
- that the 5,000 sat on green grass (6:39)
- that Jesus took little children in His arms (10:16)
- that the blind beggar was named Bartimaeus (10:46)
- that Peter recalled the curse on the fig tree (11:21)
- that the cock would crow twice before the denial (14:30)
- that on the resurrection morning the angel told the women to go tell "His disciples and Peter" (16:5)

Many other nuances of time and place also appear:

- that Jesus went to a solitary place to pray, "in the morning, rising up a great while before day" (1:35)
- that Jesus went forth to teach "by the sea side" (2:13)
- that a colt would be found "where two ways met" (11:4)
- that watching people give, "Jesus sat over against the treasury" (12:41)
- that the time of the crucifixion was "the third hour" (15:25)
- that the angel at the tomb sat "on the right side" (16:5)

Mark sees through the eyes of Peter, and with rapidity of movement reflects the apostle's vigorous nature. Peter was a man Romans everywhere would like. With rugged physique and big rough hands used to pulling heavy oars, dragging boats to shore, and hauling drooping nets full of fish, he was a man of action and energy, a natural leader transformed from clay to rock. Mark's Gospel was in substance the preaching of Peter. Some believe it was written at the request of the Romans who wanted his message in permanent form. A.T. Robertson observed that the preaching of Peter in the house of Cornelius was basically an outline of the Gospel of Mark.[3] Adapted to Roman peculiarities, this Gospel was crafted to recommend Jesus to Roman readers, the people who were the workers, conquerors, and masters of the world.

BUSYNESS

Jesus was perennially at work. Here are some more traits of Mark's style that accentuate Jesus' constant activity.

Busy days

The very first chapter records a part of a busy sabbath in Jesus' life (1:21-34). Four main incidents are listed on this day: preaching, casting out demons, healing Peter's mother-in-law, and ministering to the crowds of sick in the evening, probably to a late hour. Undoubtedly, we do not have a full accounting of all His labors that day.

This was just one of many active days in the Master's ministry. Another was the last day of Jesus' public ministry in the temple at Jerusalem. But the most bustling of all recorded days is the section, 3:19 through 5:20, which A.T. Robertson in his *Harmony of the Gospels* terms, "the Busy Day." He comments, "Observe Jesus in the forenoon teaching a crowded audience (3:19), some of whom insult and blaspheme Him, and others demand a sign, and at length His mother and brothers try to carry Him off as insane (3:21); in the afternoon giving a group of remarkable parables, several of which He interprets; towards night crossing the lake in a boat, so tired and worn that He sleeps soundly amid the alarming storm; then healing the Gadarene demoniacs, and returning by boat, apparently the same evening. What a day of toil and trial."[4]

---

3. *Studies in Mark's Gospel*, Macmillan, 1919, p. 24.
4. Harper and Brothers, 1922, p. 61.

Often Jesus was up before sunrise and still at it after sunset. On that "Busy Day" the crowds so occupied them that "they could not so much as eat bread" (3:20). Another time Jesus took the disciples apart into a desert place for a rest because the crowds gave them "no leisure so much as to eat" (6:31). Only Mark mentions that their busyness denied them eating time.

The use of "and"

English teachers do not recommend as normal practice beginning a sentence or paragraph with "and." Yet 12 of the 16 chapters in Mark (KJV) start with "and." The number of chapters commencing with "and" in the other Gospels is much smaller. The frequent use of this word, not only at the start of chapters, but throughout shows the continuous activity of the divine Servant.

Use of the historic present

Greek scholar Vincent Taylor in *The Gospels—A Short Introduction* says that "there are 151 cases of the Historic Present in Mark."[5] The Historic Present is the employment of the present tense for the purpose of relating vividly an action in the past. He goes on to say that there are parallels in only 21 cases in Matthew and but one in Luke. The other Gospels prefer to use, as a general rule, some form of the past tense, such as "He said," whereas Mark would say, "He says" (saith).

Tenney suggests that Mark's use of the historic present "creates an atmosphere of informality such as one would adopt in telling a friend about an exciting trip abroad. At the end he leaves his hearer receptive, but breathless."[6]

The use of "immediately"

"Straightway," "forthwith," and "immediately," are all translations of the same word in Greek. A favorite with Mark, this word occurs about 40 times in his Gospel, more than in all of the other books of the New Testament combined, speeding the action, and conveying promptitude in Jesus' service.

This adverb introduces the temptation of Jesus. "And immediately the Spirit driveth Him into the wilderness" (1:12). Matthew

---

5. The Epworth Press, no date, p. 39.
6. *The Genius of the Gospels*, p. 82.

and Luke say that Jesus was led by the Spirit into the wilderness, but only Mark tells us that He was driven, imparting a sense of urgency in keeping with a servant's status.

On a visit to Hammond Castle Museum in Gloucester, Massachusetts, I heard the tour guide say that in Gothic times a servant would sleep at the foot of his master's bed, so as to be available for immediate obedience to any command. This reminds us of David's words, "The king's business requireth haste" (1 Sam. 21:8).

SERVANTHOOD

In his book, *Mark: The Servant Gospel*, Donald Grey Barnhouse wrote, "Certainly Jesus' supernatural power and authority are evident. But His heavenly glory and majesty are veiled. We see Jesus as a servant in constant, tireless ministry to endless need." [7] Preeminently Mark portrays Jesus as Servant.

Mark omits the fanfare at his birth. Henrietta Mears suggests that "the skill of an artist may lie in what he leaves out. An amateur crowds everything in." Significant in Mark's portrait of Jesus as a servant are his omissions: no mention of His birth, no choir of angels, no adoration of shepherds, no wise men worshiping a king, no twelve-year-old lad confounding the temple doctors, no description of angels as "His" angels (Matt. 24:31), but just "the" angels (13:27), and no commanding power over angels, though angels did minister to Him (1:13).

Mark has no genealogy. Through the years I have filled in countless recommendations for young people wishing to go to college, or seeking employment. Not once have I been asked to vouch for an applicant's family tree. Though aliens may be required to prove USA residency, pedigree is not required for employment. A servant need not produce his genealogy.

Fitness of Mark's occupation

By occupation Mark was suited to pen Jesus' servanthood. His only occupation mentioned is that of a servant. Paul and Barnabas took him along in that capacity on their first journey (Acts 13:5). His job description may have included travel arrangements, lodging places, and vehicle conveyances. Would they choose Trans Turkey or Antioch Amtrack? Because Mark defected in the early part of the

---

7. Victor Books, 1988, in chapter, "The Life of a Servant."

trip, Paul refused to let Barnabas bring him on a proposed second trip. So Barnabas took Mark as his helper, while Paul chose Silas and went another way. But a dozen or so years later Paul asked Timothy to bring Mark, who by this time had proven himself worthy for service (2 Tim. 4:11). Again Mark became a servant to Paul. Apparently Mark also served in the same capacity to Peter (1 Peter 5:13).

The one who wrote of Jesus as Servant was himself a servant. Not an apostle, but the servant of apostles. Mark is the only Gospel which gives Jesus' occupation—carpenter (6:3), though Matthew terms Him the carpenter's son. Matthew seems interested in Joseph's job; Mark stresses Jesus' vocation.

Unostentatious

When as a child I made too much noise, my mother would say, "Little children are to be seen, not heard." Could not the same be said of servants? Jesus certainly modeled the self-effacement of a servant, never seeking to be conspicuous. Rather He seemed to seek anonymity. This may be why Mark has so many references to Jesus entering a house. He wanted to shun publicity (2:1; 3:19; 7:17, 24; 9:28, 33). To escape the adulation of the surging crowds He often withdrew to a mountain spot, a desert place, or a quiet seaside to be with either His disciples or His heavenly Father (e.g., 1:35-38; 1:45; 3:7-12). He played it low key.

To perform two of His miracles He took the ill men aside for the healing. One, a deaf man with a speech impediment, He took away from the multitude, minimizing the man's embarrassment at first attempts to speak, as well as avoiding the limelight for Himself. In fact, "He charged them that they should tell no man: but the more He charged them, so much the more a great deal they published it" (7:36).

The second case, a blind man, he led out of town. After restoring his sight, "He sent him away to his house, saying, Neither go into the town, nor tell it to any in the town" (8:26).

He went about the villages teaching (6:6). Perhaps He preferred the unobtrusive, quiet village ministry to the glare of more public towns. Another reason for His retirements was to renew His strength for the next task. After the strain of vigorous labor He said to the disciples, "Come ye . . . apart, . . . and rest awhile" (6:31, 32). Perfectly integrated, He balanced busy activity with prayerful rest. He knew that frenzied busyness ultimately is a drag, whereas a proper pause refreshes.

To paint servant-modesty Mark sometimes omits or downgrades titles used in other Gospels. Matthew has the disciples awakening Jesus in the storm, "Lord, save us: we perish" (8:25). But Mark reports them as arousing Him, "Master, carest Thou not that we perish?" (4:38). The "Lord" of Matthew looms superior to the "Master" of Mark. In many modern versions "Master" is translated "Teacher." Compare Matthew 16:22 with Mark 8:32, Matthew 17:4 with Mark 9:5, Matthew 26:22 with Mark 14:19.

Less talking

Missing in Mark is the Sermon on the Mount which comprises three chapters in Matthew. Though Mark has Jesus doing His share of teaching, he gives only four full-fledged parables, this in contrast to Matthew with 20 parables. A king, as in Matthew, speaks. A servant, as in Mark, works. So Mark relates about 20 miracles, but only four parables, all of which deal with workers sowing seed (4:3-20; 4:26-29; 4:30-32; 12:1-12). Doesn't a servant major in deeds, not words? Some Bible students add a fifth parable, found only in Mark (13:33 37), which urges servants to be ready for the master's return. Unsurprisingly, Matthew's parable of the king's son (22:1-14) is omitted in Mark.

A servant often has to bear a message. Since "gospel," means "good news," it seems significant that the word "gospel," which occurs 12 times in the four Gospels, is found eight of those occasions in Mark. Servant Jesus came announcing good news.

Uses His eyes

A cartoon showed a woman sick in bed, obviously in pain. The sink was stacked with dishes. Clothes to be ironed were piled nearby. Two dirty-faced little children were scrapping in the corner. And a dog was munching on some food it had knocked from the table. A smiling neighbor stands in the doorway. The caption under the cartoon has her say, "Well, Mary, if there's anything I can do to help, don't hesitate to let me know."

The most casual look should have suggested ways to help. So often Jesus used His eyes to take in a situation. Mainly in Mark we find mention of Jesus beholding, seeing, or looking around:

- at the Pharisees objecting to a Sabbath healing   (3:5)
- at His mother and brothers   (3:34)
- at the woman who touched the hem of His garment   (5:32)
- at the disciples trying to prevent mothers from bringing their little ones to Him. Only Mark mentions that He saw this   (10:14)
- at the rich young ruler   (10:21)
- at His disciples when the rich young ruler left   (10:23)
- at His disciples astonished at His saying about the difficulty of the rich entering the kingdom   (10:27)
- at the temple in Jerusalem   (11:11)

Guests at an exclusive dinner on Barbados in a room where the Queen of England had once dined, my wife and I thoroughly enjoyed the eight-course meal. Since we did not wish the wines, we wanted tea. But how to get it? Looking up about the time I wished my beverage, I saw my waiter across the room looking in my direction. Immediately his eyes made contact with mine, and in a moment he was by my side to take my request. And in no time my wife and I had our tea. His alert eyes had seen our need.

Had the disciples looked around the Upper Room the night of the Passover, they would have seen the basin of water and towel, and realized the need for someone to do the foot-washing. The Psalmist speaks of a servant keeping "his eyes upon his master . . . for the slightest signal" (123:2, LL). The ideal servant looks with his eyes to see what needs to be done, then uses his hands to fill that need.

Uses His hands

According to the *Wall St. Journal*, there are models whose hands appear in TV commercials and magazine ads, never their faces. These hands may be pouring, touching, pushing, pointing, squeezing or rubbing. One hand model found himself holding rats for a breeder of laboratory animals. A few hands earn six-figure incomes. For the money, advertisers demand perfection. Cameras zoom in so close that ordinary hands become hideous, and thumbnails loom as big as the TV screen. An ever-so-thin paper cut can knock a model out of business for days or weeks, as can a jagged nail, shaggy cuticle, or blackened thumb. Some models insure their hands through Lloyd's of London. Many settle for less costly protection by wearing gloves, even to bed after gooking on oils and creams. Sunbathing is taboo, unless, of course, the model wears gloves on the beach.

No hands were ever so valuable and powerful as those of Jesus. Though all Gospels mention Jesus touching the sick, Mark makes more frequent mention of His hands, often where the others are silent. Observantly looking around with His eyes and spotting needs, He goes to work with His hands. He sees, then does.

Mark, telling of unbelief in Nazareth adds, "He could there do no mighty work, save that He laid His hands upon a few sick folk, and healed them" (6:2, 5). Matthew, the only other Gospel to record this event, omits any mention of His hands (13:54).

Mark, only one to relate the healing of the deaf man with a speech impediment, tells how the deaf man's friends begged Jesus "to put His hand upon him," and how Jesus "put His fingers into his ears, and He spit, and touched his tongue" (7:32, 33).

Mark, again the only Gospel to record the healing of the blind man of Bethsaida, states that the people asked Jesus to touch the victim. Then also, how He had to touch him twice to restore his sight fully, because after the first touch he saw only dimly, "men as trees, walking" (8:22-25).

Though three Gospels report the healing of a demon-possessed son, only Mark tells us that "Jesus took him by the hand, and lifted him up" (9:27; Matt. 17:14-20; Luke 9:37-43).

In his Transfiguration account Matthew says that Jesus' face shone as the sun. One author says that since the sun is viewed universally as "the king of the day," Matthew gives us a kingly description of Jesus. [8] Mark does not mention His shining face, but adds that His garments became whiter than anyone could possibly bleach them (9:3). Whose responsibility but a servant's to keep his master's garment spotlessly white? Did Mark have the servant's hands in mind?

Some early doctors in Hawaii could not bring themselves to touch lepers. One used to set his medicines out on his gate post so that they would not have to come near him. Another on his rounds of the leprosy hospital would do physical examinations by raising the rags from a diseased body with the tip of his cane. One minister preached to the lepers from the elevated distance of a veranda; he

---

8. F.D. Van Valkenburgh, *Why Four Gospels?*, Pentecostal Publishing Co., Louisville, KY, 1915, p. 55.

would not touch the objects of his professed concern. But the lepers did not take their doctoring or preaching seriously, for they needed to touch and be touched. Happily, later doctors and missionaries showed their compassion by personal touching, affirming their common humanity.

Prompted by love

Though all Gospels highlight the love of Jesus, Mark sometimes mentions it where others omit it. In the incident of Jesus blessing the children, only Mark says that He took the little ones in His arms, certainly a touch which reflects the Savior's warmth (10:16; Matt. 19:13-15; Luke 18:15-17).

In the healing of the leper, only Mark says Jesus was moved with compassion (1:41; Matt. 8:2-4; Luke 5:12-16).

In the story of the rich young ruler who came to Jesus, then went away, only Mark adds, "Jesus beholding him loved him" (10:21; Matt. 19:16-22; Luke 18:18-23).

Our service, too, must be motivated by love, else it will be like banging gongs. Our Sunday school teaching, church attendance, choir singing, visitation, apart from love, will be monotonous drudgery. We'll become professional, going through the routines, like the man described in a *Reader's Digest* picturesque speech column as "nothing behind his smile but teeth."

A group of American believers, after attending a conference of Christians behind what was then the Iron Curtain, spent the night with a widower, a retired layman who had been deeply moved by the sessions. He welcomed the group with two basins of water and some towels, washed their feet, and loaned them slippers while he shined their shoes. He fed them with delicacies far beyond his budget, and insisted on serving them, all the time resisting repeated pleas to sit with them at the table. Unable to speak English, he tied a towel to his belt and pointed to the Bible, doubtless to remind his guests of Jesus' servant role. Periodically during the evening and even after the guests were in bed, their host slipped outside to make sure their car had not been vandalized. At dawn he was outside, washing the car. He served a lavish breakfast, and packed food for several days. Said a guest, "I don't know how far removed in heaven I shall be from Christ's glorious throne, but I expect that, after the martyrs, he'll be numbered among the self-giving saints of God."

Rejected

But the Servant was not appreciated. As predicted, He was rejected, plotted against, betrayed, arrested, forsaken, denied, falsely condemned, spat on, buffeted, crowned with thorns, mocked, crucified, and buried. He had come, not only to serve, but to give His life a ransom. That was His ultimate service.

But death could not keep its prey. Jesus rose triumphant over death and over His enemies. He appeared to His disciples and taught them for forty days. Then He ascended into heaven. Mark ends with a striking statement. Though not found in the earliest manuscripts, how fitting this ending, namely that the disciples "went forth, and preached everywhere, the Lord *working* with them" (16:20). The portrait of a servant is maintained to the end—the risen Jesus is still working away, working with His disciples who have gone forth, likewise serving.

A daughter recalls from earliest years her mother often saying, "Remember, dear, you have not been placed on earth just to please yourself. You have been sent by God to serve others." That girl became a welfare worker, devoting her career to improving the lives of the materially poor and spiritually needy.

Today as we serve in His vineyard, we do not work alone. We have a faithful, heavenly Coworker. The same Servant who ministered in Judea and Galilee works with us and through us to accomplish His purposes. Since believers are called "servants" about 60 times in the New Testament, Mark's portrait should help us learn how to become good servants of Jesus Christ.

6

Learning to Serve

The pastor of a thriving church spoke of an old shoemaker, a friend of many years. As a young seminarian, the pastor had been poor, and also found his courses a struggle. But he had been given constant encouragement and financial help by the shoemaker. When he finally finished his training, and was about to be ordained, the shoemaker said, "I have a favor to ask. When I was your age, I wanted to be a preacher, but things didn't work out. You have been given the task that I was never able to do. I want you to let me make your shoes—at no charge. Then when you are in your pulpit, I will think of you standing in the shoes I made, preaching the gospel in a way I'll never have the chance to do."

The shoemaker demonstrated the servant spirit. But this temperament does not come naturally. Human nature finds it easier to grab than to give, and more convenient to be served than to serve. But Jesus exemplified the attitude of a servant, sketched in Mark's Gospel. The Master wants His followers to develop the same disposition. Here are helps to servanthood.

PONDER THE CONDESCENSION OF JESUS

Several times since 1983 newspapers have carried feature stories

71

of former President Jimmy Carter and his wife, Rosalyn, donning dungarees to work in some blighted inner city area, as volunteers for Habitat for Humanity which provides housing for the needy. Carter's picture often shows him hammering on a house under construction, while his wife pitches in with a shovel to help with landscaping. I never cease to be impressed by such a seeming come-down—from President to carpenter, from oval office to inner city, from influential white-collar job to menial blue-collar labor. One headline read, "Working Class Carters."

Infinitely greater condescension was displayed by the Lord of heaven in His coming to earth two thousand years ago. The re-splendent Second Person of the Trinity surrendered His glory. He who was Deity became man. The Somebody of heaven made Him-self a nobody on earth. Many men in high office like to be known as president of the company or chairman of the board. But the Lord Jesus did not count the prestige of equality with God such a fascina-tion that it had to be tenaciously retained or conspicuously spot-lighted.

Near the close of a 1946 graduation exercise at the University of Pennsylvania, at which I had just received a degree, the monotony was suddenly broken when the name of a five-star general was called out as the recipient of an honorary degree. From his seat near the back, General Hap Arnold marched down the aisle, erect, with dignity, and wearing all the medals of his top-brass position. Had he been dressed as a civilian, and named without rank, few of us would have noticed. The Son of God, infinitely higher than any five-star general, came to earth without His insignia showing. Peo-ple, passing Him on a road, didn't have the slightest inkling of His exalted personage. It was said of Him, "There standeth One among you, whom ye know not." He served unostentatiously. When those He healed wished to broadcast His exploits He ordered them not to tell. Most VPs would have shifted their publicity machines into high gear. Yet He humbled Himself, not coming as a bigwig. With-out giving up His deity, He threw off the outer trappings of His Godhead.

When the Salvation Army was beginning to make its mark to-ward the end of the last century, people from other parts of the world came to England to enlist. One American prelate, whose ambition had once been to become a bishop, left a thriving pastor-ate, and crossed the Atlantic to enlist. General Booth was reluctant to accept him, pointing out that in his army soldiers were under the orders of superiors and, "You've been your own boss too long." But he took Samuel Brengle on probation, and to teach him humility, assigned him the job of cleaning the shoes of other trainees. The discouraged Brengle wondered, "Have I followed my own fancy across the Atlantic just to black boots?" Then, in his mind, he saw Jesus bending over the feet of rough, untutored, bumbling Galileans. He whispered, "Lord, You washed their feet. I will black their shoes." Then as he bent over those dirty boots, motivated by the condescension of Jesus, he began to learn servanthood. Brengle, learning his lesson well, lived a life of serving, and became the Army's first American-born commissioner. [1]

REVIEW THE TEACHING OF JESUS

My daughter, a lawyer in Washington and her husband, a financial adviser also in the capital, like many working couples had trouble juggling work and home responsibilities. One Saturday, discussing who should do a certain job, they began to argue mildly over who worked the harder, and who had the more important role. Suddenly their seven-year-old daughter whispered softly, "Mother, may I see you privately in the bedroom?" When the door was closed, little Caroline asked, "Mother, do you remember teaching the lesson last year about the disciples arguing over who was the greatest?" (My daughter is her Sunday school teacher.) Her question opened my daughter's eyes. She went out and told her husband who said, "Caroline is right!" That ended the discussion.

The Twelve often argued among themselves who would be number one in the coming kingdom. One time their ambition-laden dispute incongruously followed their Master's disclosure of His coming betrayal and killing. When He asked them what they had been arguing about, they were too ashamed to tell. He sat down and taught, "If any man desire to be first, the same shall be last of all, and servant of all." To reinforce His teaching, He gave them an object lesson. He placed a child in the midst, saying that real greatness lies in the humility that would service the needs of the lowliest and feeblest, like that of a little child (Mk. 9:31-37).

Despite Jesus' instruction the Twelve's competitive spirit persist-

---

1. Kent and Barbara Hughes, *Liberating Ministry from the Success Syndrome*, Tyndale, 1987, p. 45.

ed. Before the final trip to Jerusalem James and John aspired through their mother's intervention to the two top seats in the kingdom. When the ten heard, they were indignant with the two brothers, exchanging angry glances and words. Jesus called them together and said, in effect, "You know that heathen rulers like to be number one so they can exercise authority over people. But not so with you. Whoever wants to be chief shall be servant of all" (Mk. 10:35-44). What proves a person great is not that others wait on him, but that he waits on others. The measure of a person is not how many serve him, but how many he serves. Then, to offset the lofty attitude of His disciples, He introduced the example of His own lowly service, "For even the Son of man came not to be ministered unto, but to minister, and to give his life a ransom for many" (vs. 45), the key verse of Mark.

But they still had not learned the lesson. At the passover celebration in the Upper Room they were still at it. With their Master's cross less than twenty-four hours away, the reclining disciples again inappropriately argued among themselves as to who should rank the highest. Again the Master patiently admonished them that though heathen rulers bossed their subjects around, His followers should act the opposite. Whoever is chief should serve. He asked—who is the more important at a meal, the one who sits and is served, or the one who does the serving? The usual answer would be—the one who sits and is waited on. His reply is so radical and mind-boggling, "I am among you as he that serveth." Then by graphic performance of a lowly task He demonstrated that He was a servant (Lk. 22:24-27).

At this point, according to many scholars, Jesus rose to take a servant's role. Common courtesy called for a host to wash the soiled feet of arriving guests. Because the upper room was borrowed, no host was present to take care of the usual ablutions. But basin and towel had been thoughtfully provided. Who would do the honors? With atmosphere charged with feverish wish to be number one, no aspiring leader would abdicate his throne of ambition to kneel before his supposed subjects. Looking away from the towel and basin with studied indifference, each regarded this task below his dignity. Amazingly, Jesus rose and picked up the basin and towel. The Lord of Glory—at whose beckon legions of angels were ready to serve—chose the servant's place, taking the soiled feet in His own hands.

When He had gone the rounds, He gave an unforgettable command, "If I then, your Lord and Master, have washed your feet; ye also ought to wash one another's feet. For I have given you an example, that ye should do as I have done to you" (John 13:14, 15). Though the Lord may not have established a foot-washing ordinance, none can escape the clear injunction to serve others in need, even those on a lower social scale.

Jesus served in various ways. He taught publicly to the crowds and privately to groups. He healed. He broke bread and handed it to His disciples. He replenished the refreshments at the wedding in Cana. He broke bread at the Last Supper. In the Emmaus home after the resurrection He who was guest became host. On the seashore appearance to His disciples He prepared the breakfast, inviting them to "Come and dine." Peter described Him as one "who went about doing good, and healing all that were oppressed of the devil" (Acts 10:38). The Lord of Glory served!

So strongly did the example of Christ's service dominate early Christian thinking that the titles given their leaders signify service. A minister is simply one who ministers or serves—a servant. The word "deacon" comes from a verb which means to "minister" or "serve." A pastor is a servant-shepherd of the flock. A bishop is an overseeing servant. Paul called himself "a servant of Jesus Christ" (Rom. 1:1). When the Corinthian church caused divisions by lining up behind favorite leaders, Paul reminded them all those leaders were but servants of the Master. Church leaders are not bosses but servants.

At the final rehearsal for the coronation of Queen Elizabeth the orchestra had just finished its last number. The archbishop stood erect by the altar, and nearby in ranks stood officers of the state. Suddenly a spine-tingling fanfare of trumpets burst forth, the signal for the entrance of the queen. But instead, when the massive doors opened, in trotted four servant girls pushing carpet sweepers. They nonchalantly proceeded to circle the throne, removing stray feathers and fuzz which had floated onto the golden carpet. These maids had their place. Their lowly service was needed to prevent a sovereign's or statesman's sneeze. But no one would have crowned any of those maids as queen. At most, believers are unprofitable servants.

BE WILLING TO DO LOWLY TASKS

The late Shoichiro Honda, the automobile maker whose company was the first to use American workers to build Japanese cars, was installed in the Automotive Hall of Fame in October 1989, to join Henry Ford, Walter Chrysler and other distinguished car builders. *The New York Times* reported that through the years Honda often dressed in the clothes of an assembly line worker and left work covered with grease. The article recounted that for relaxation Honda turned into a party animal. Once at a party when a drunken guest accidentally flushed his dentures down the toilet, Honda volunteered to climb into the septic tank to find them. "The next day, at a party thrown to celebrate retrieval of the dentures, Honda said his actions had proved an important point: The chief executive should be ready to perform the lowliest task before asking one of his subordinates to do it" (10/9/89).

Management consultant Robert Greenleaf in his books, *Servant Leadership*, and *The Servant as Religious Leader*, demonstrates the distinct superiority of servant leadership over the more self-serving forms of leadership. How do you tell if you are a servant leader? The answer comes in whether you give the highest priority to meeting your own needs or the needs of other people. Do those you serve grow as individuals? And the effect on the least privileged in society must be taken into consideration—they must benefit, or, at least, not be further deprived, if you are to qualify as a servant-leader. Meanness of work never lowers a person. Rather, the spiritual law of rank says the higher you wish to stand, the lower you must stoop to serve.

Late one evening during a conference at Moody Bible Institute D. L. Moody on a walk around the halls came upon the guest rooms where visiting English preachers were sleeping. Outside each door was a pair of shoes. Moody recalled the European practice of putting one's shoes outside the door on retiring to be polished by the host before morning. Spotting some students down the hall, Moody explained the custom and asked, "Would you fellows get a piece of chalk, put the number of the room on the soles of the shoes, then shine them nicely?" One student protested, "Mr. Moody, I didn't come here to clean shoes. I came here to study to be a preacher." When the others said the same, Moody dismissed them to their rooms, collected the shoes himself, polished them nicely, and put them back in place.

Somehow shining shoes has come to symbolize humble service. Recently a picture in our local paper showed New York State Governor Mario Cuomo shining the shoes of the man who had been bootblack for twenty-five years at a stock exchange on Wall St. Cuomo had given a speech, had his shoes shined, then with brush in hand was playing turnabout. On Holy Thursday the Pope makes a practice of washing the feet of down-and-outers brought in from Rome's slums. But there are many ways of lowly service.

A Pullman porter became friendly with a Christian businessman. One night as the train pulled into Boston, the porter related that he had a hard-working mother who wanted to see her two boys receive a good education. His desire was to enter the ministry, but to earn money he became a railroad porter. As he saved money, his younger brother drank, partied, and nearly lost his life in profligate living. Just as the porter was accepted for college, his brother was converted, felt a call to the ministry, and asked for financial help. The porter, knowing his brother had nothing, and delighted at the change in his life, put him through college. The brother became a nationally known preacher through his radio ministry. Asked the porter, "My brother has led thousands to Christ. As you see, I couldn't go into the ministry, and I'm too old now. Do you suppose the Lord will give me some credit for the souls my brother won?" He was assured that his faithful, day-by-day, menial labor would not go unrewarded. Those who stay by the stuff will share with those who go down to battle.

An infidel became a Christian after an auto mishap. He explained, "After the accident a limousine stopped, and a lady got out and walked toward me. I was staggering around, covered with blood. When she caught me by the arm, I instinctively cried out that I was bleeding, and not to come nearer because I would get her dirty. She had her chauffeur come and lift me into the back seat of her limousine. When I complained of the mess my blood would make, she said, 'What's a dress! What's upholstery! You're hurt!' It was this gesture that broke my heart." To be a servant requires reaching out to people without looking to see if their hands are bloody or dirty.

One of the most moving missionary biographies concerns a Belgian priest, Joseph Damien, who at thirty-three volunteered to spend the rest of his life on the island of Molokai, where lepers were abandoned to their terrible fate without comfort. He found the victims a hideous sight: faces with ugly holes where eyes had been, rotting mouths, ears often swollen many times their size, hands without fingers, feet merely stumps, and covered with open revolting sores. He repeatedly fought back the temptation to vomit or faint. For sixteen years he lived among them, washing their wounds, holding their maggot-infested limbs, changing their bandages, sharing his plate of food. He built them better houses, a better church building, and a better water supply. He buried their dead, personally digging more than 2,000 graves, and conducted a funeral almost every day. He later died, a leper himself.

The servant image is indelibly portrayed by Victor Herman, an American imprisoned in Soviet Russia's Gulag for 45 years, in his autobiography, *Coming Out of the Ice*. He was first jailed in Cell 39, a space five-and-a-half feet wide and ten feet long with a boarded-up window at the far end. Along each wall were two benches on which sixteen men sat. Next to the door was a round vat, called a Parasha, a latrine with a choking stench and emptied every ten days. The men were forbidden to talk or move. From dawn to dark they stared at the hole in the cell door. At night they lay on the cold stone, every corner of space occupied. The slightest move to relieve a pain disturbed others. The prisoners would have gone mad but for "the Elder," a cellmate who sat closest to the latrine, where the smell was the most pungent, and nearest the door, exposing him to the mindless blows of the guards. The Elder counted out sixteen bowls of soup as they came through the hole in the cell door to make sure each prisoner received his share, and to allow no one to start eating till all were served. Twice each night he gave a signal for the men to change sleeping positions to prevent cramping. But for the Elder the men would have fought for food and space. James R. Edwards comments, "Cell 39 will remain a model of Christian service for me for a long time . . . Only the person who sits closest to the parasha, as it were, and who is most exposed to the blows of the system, can claim authority to lead and serve. The authority of a servant stands in inverse proportion to his claims for himself." [2]

Philip Yancey wrote in his column in *Christianity Today*, "My career as a journalist has afforded me opportunities to interview diverse people. Looking back, I can roughly divide them into two types: stars and servants. The stars include NFL football greats, movie actors, music performers, famous authors, TV personalities, and the like. These are the ones who dominate our magazines and our television programs, too. We fawn over them, poring over the minutia of their lives: the clothes they wear, the food they eat, the

---

2. "The Calling" in *Christianity Today*, p. 66.

aerobic routines they follow, the people they love, the places they go, the toothpaste they use." He adds that these are miserable people, many with troubled marriages, dependent on psychothera-py, and tormented by self-doubt.

Then he mentioned that he had also spent time with servants, like a doctor who worked twenty years among outcast leprosy pa-tients in rural India, or health-workers who left high-paying posi-tions to serve with Mendenhall Ministries in Mississippi, or relief workers in Africa, or Ph.D.'s scattered throughout foreign jungles translating the Bible into obscure languages. He concluded, "But as I now reflect on the two groups, stars and servants, the servants clearly emerge as the favored ones, the graced ones. They work for low pay, long hours and no applause, 'wasting' their talents and skills among the poor and uneducated. But somehow in the process of losing their lives, they have found them." [3]

Pure religion involves visitation of the fatherless and widows in their affliction (James 1:27). In the day of judgment the blessed will be rewarded for feeding the hungry, taking in the homeless, cloth-ing the cold, and visiting the sick and prisoners (Matt. 25:34-36). The parable of the Good Samaritan teaches that service should extend to anyone in need that crosses our path. Even the insignifi-cant favor of a cup of cold water in Jesus' name will not go unre-warded (Mk. 9:41).

MAKE TIME FOR SERVING

The parable of the Good Samaritan was re-enacted, not on the road from Jerusalem to Jericho, but on a street in Princeton, NJ. Two psychologists recruited forty students from Princeton Semi-nary for an experiment. Half of the seminarians were asked to prepare a talk on the parable of the Good Samaritan, while the other half were given a different subject. Then one by one, at fifteen-minute intervals, they were told to go to another building to record their talk. Each found on his way, lying in a doorway in the alley, a young man coughing and groaning in seeming pain. The "victim" had been put there by the psychologist to see if the semi-narians would play the role of the Good Samaritan or pass him by. Particularly, would those on the way to record a talk on the Good Samaritan stop? Of the forty students, sixteen stopped to help.

---

3. "Low Pay, Long Hours, No Applause," Nov. 18, 1988, p. 80.

Twenty-four did not. What determined whether a man stopped or passed by? It had nothing to do with whether or not he had prepared a talk on the Good Samaritan. The psychologists had introduced another factor. They told some of the boys they would be early for their recording; some, that it was time to go; and others, that they were already late, hinting that they should rush. The low hurry group had the highest percentage who stopped to help. Those in the intermediate hurry group had the next highest percentage. But those in the high hurry group had the smallest percentage. The conclusion—one's readiness to help did not depend on the subject on his mind, nor on the condition of his soul, but on whether or not he was in a hurry. The parable's priest and Levite were probably in a hurry because of other priorities, while the Samaritan had fewer people depending on him to be at a certain place at a certain time.

If we are to develop the servant attitude, we will have to make it one of our priorities. One couple said, "Not so long ago we used our free time just like other folks, took another job, watched TV, puttered around the yard. We weren't deeply involved in our church life. Now we open up our home for young people. We go on retreats as advisors. We are usually available."

Many tasks await those who will take time to serve. Seniors need rides to church. Underprivileged need tutoring. Refugees need help in adjusting to our culture. Parents of handicapped children welcome a few hours of relief. One fellow devoted several evening hours each week to maintain church property. A stockbroker spent Saturday mornings phoning new residents, giving both an invitation to church and a gospel witness, resulting in several families joining the church. The vice-president of a Wall Street bank took time four evenings a week, after a hard day's work in the city and a weary commuter's ride to his New Jersey community, to act as a volunteer orderly in a nearby veteran's hospital. He fed, washed, and readied disabled soldiers for bed.

A little known sidelight in the career of the distinguished apologist and Princeton Seminary professor Dr. J. Gresham Machen occurred during World War I. Applying for service with the overseas YMCA, he was first assigned the lowly task of manufacturing and selling a hot chocolate drink in a French village. The involved process meant rising much earlier to open the canteen at 7 a.m., and postponing his breakfast till after 9 a.m. Though he wished for heavier responsibility, especially in the area of his profession, this ordained, scholarly professor was content with the opportunity to perform menial service for months. But during the latter part of his yearlong sojourn in France he enjoyed numerous opportunities to preach the gospel.

Henri Nouwen, a Dutch diocesan priest, has spent nearly two decades in North America, teaching in schools like Notre Dame and Yale. In the eighties he left his post at Harvard to go to a community called Daybreak, near Toronto, Canada. There he spends hours daily taking care of a twenty-four-year-old man who cannot speak, does not cry or laugh, cannot dress himself, walk alone, or eat without much help. His arm and leg movements are twisted. He suffers epileptic seizures almost daily. It takes an hour and a half to wake him up, medicate, bathe, shave, dress, give him breakfast, place him in his wheelchair and push him to the therapy room for his daily exercises. Spending hours with this young man which many would consider a vegetable, Nouwen has come to see what a violently competitive work he has left behind. By taking time out to serve in this lowly way, he has come to realize how his earlier life was driven by desire for success in the academic world and in Christian ministry.

STIR THE FLAME OF DEVOTION

Because Jesus stooped to serve us, we should stoop in lowly ministry to others. Our sense of debt should urge us to unpretentious, faithful service. Out of gratitude for His grace that redeemed us from our guilt, we should gladly succor those in distress. Without this response of love, the zeal for service may flicker and fade. The flame of devotion must be kept alive. We can serve without loving, but we cannot love without serving.

But how do we fan the flame of devotion? Paul, exhorting the Philippians to unselfish service, reminded them of the self-emptying ministry of Jesus. He wrote, "Let this mind be in you, which was also in Christ Jesus" (2:5). He outlined the steps of Jesus' condescension—from God to man, to nobody, to servant, to the shameful death of the cross, so horrible a death it was reserved for criminals, foreigners, and slaves. Though his humiliation was followed by His victorious exaltation, meditating often on His sacrifice will lead us to present our bodies a living sacrifice. Love so amazing, so divine, demands our life, our soul, our all.

The late Dr. Eric Frykenberg, a missionary who spent half a century in India, could regale friends with incidents of his life on the field. Once someone asked, "What was the most difficult problem you ever faced?" Without hesitation he answered, "It was when my heart would grow cold before God. When that happened, I knew I was too busy. I also knew it was time to get away. So I would take my Bible and go off into the hills alone. I'd open my Bible to the story of the crucifixion and I would wrap my arms around the Cross. And then I'd be ready to go back to work."

The *Clergy Journal* used to carry a monthly column titled "Dear Amicus," a ministerial parallel to "Ann Landers." One letter came from an unhappy senior pastor. At a recent church function, because of shortage of chairs, someone had asked him to get some chairs to set up at the back of the room. Though he did it, he was deeply offended. He wrote, "Don't they know who I am? The senior pastor of a large metropolitan church should not be expected to carry chairs like a common custodian." Amicus wrote back, "Dear Disgusted, have you forgotten that we are followers of Him who came not to be served but to serve?"

Even when we have served our best, we are still unworthy servants.

7

Particularly in Luke

A one-page article in *Newsweek* depicted the plight of children with AIDS. Prominently displayed, the picture of a poster showed a child with arms outstretched pleading, "I have AIDS. Please hug me. I can't make you sick."

Had he lived in our century, Dr. Luke, author of the third Gospel, would no doubt have expressed genuine pity toward victims of AIDS, whether child or adult. He would have been reflecting the sympathy which characterized the ministry of the Lord Jesus Christ toward the despised and outcasts of life. Of the four Gospel writers Luke is the one who emphasizes the manhood of Jesus and, through numerous tender episodes, mirrors His compassionate kinship with humanity.

These words sum up Luke's Gospel: Gentile, humanity, compassion.

GENTILE

A Greek author

A high-schooler in a Sunday school quiz said that the Gospels were written by Matthew, Mark, Luther, and John. Though Luke was the author of the third Gospel, like Luther he may have been a Gentile (Col. 4:10-14). If so, he may have been the only Gentile author of any Bible book. As a physician, he possessed a superior education, and as a writer he displayed a mature literary flourish. He directed his Gospel to a Greek of eminent position—"most excellent Theophilus"—who would be capable of admiring his well-crafted, thoroughly researched, orderly history, with a style more polished than both the didactic approach of Matthew and the street-preaching technique of Mark.

Luke wrote with the Greeks in mind

Luke did not employ his literary talents only for rational impact or artistic effect. He wanted to use his cultured manner to exalt the One Who was both Son of God and Son of Man. Luke blended various traits of Jesus into a charming picture that appealed to the Greek mind—the portrait of a perfect man. Historians generally agree that the Greeks reached the summit of intellectual accomplishment with the philosophies of Plato and Aristotle a few centuries B.C. The arts also then flourished in Greek society, giving us the highest and noblest expressions of human endeavor. The Greeks were striving for the ideal man. So Luke presents to them Jesus Christ as the model and pinnacle of humanity, the mightiest and the holiest, the man without a flaw, THE MAN of all men. Though strong, Jesus wept. A meek man, He radiated courage. In the midst of kindhearted teaching He called Herod a fox. Mixing tough and tender, Luke portrayed a sinless man, altogether lovely, deeply sympathetic, in Whom judgment and mercy, truth and love, perfectly fused together.

The Greeks represent the human race at large

Though Luke was written with the Greeks in mind, the Greeks stand for Gentiles everywhere. Not universalism (everyone will be saved), but universality (the gospel is for all peoples) is suggested several times through the Gospel. All national barriers are down; no prejudice exists in Luke's writing.

A hard lesson for the early church was the admission of Gentiles into the church unless they kept the Mosaic law. Luke hints at this Gentile inclusion in reporting Simeon's Song which called the baby "A light to lighten the Gentiles" (2:32).

Though Matthew, Mark and Luke all quote Isaiah 40:3 as a prophecy of John the Baptist's ministry, only Luke goes on to quote verse 5 which predicts an outreach to the Gentiles, "And all flesh shall see the salvation of God" (3:6).

Luke records Jesus' favorable references to Gentiles in His sermon in hometown Nazareth. Despite the plight of widows in Israel during a famine, Elijah was sent by God, not to Israeli widows, but to a Gentile widow in the Sidon city of Sarepta. Though many lepers lived in Israel during the days of Elisha, none was cleansed, except Naaman, the Syrian (4:25-27). These Gentiles were examples of divine favor beyond Israeli borders.

When Jesus sent out the Twelve, according to Matthew He instructed them not to go into the way of the Gentiles or Samaritans, but rather to the lost sheep of the house of Israel (10:5,6). But neither Luke nor Mark report this prohibition.

Matthew gives the parable of the fig tree, which typifies Israel (24:32, 33). But Luke recounts Jesus speaking not only of the fig tree, but of "all the trees" (21:29, 30). H. A. Ironside suggests that "all the trees" refers "to the Gentile nations." [1] Only in Luke are we informed that Jerusalem shall be trodden down "of the Gentiles, until the times of the Gentiles be fulfilled" (21:24).

Only Luke designates the site of Jesus' crucifixion by its Gentile name, Calvary (23:33). He changes Jewish terminology so that scribes become lawyers; Rabbi is Master; and the Sea of Galilee is known as Lake Gennesaret.

Though Matthew and Mark both contain the Great Commission to all the world and to every creature, Luke states the command, "Repentance and remission of sins should be preached in His name among all nations, beginning in Jerusalem" (24:47). "Nations" refers to non-Jewish races, sometimes translated "Gentiles." In the sequel to his Gospel, the book of Acts, Luke traces the history of missions from Jerusalem to Samaria, to Caesarea, to Antioch, to Asia Minor, to Greece, and to Rome. Some scholars suggest that Luke intended to pen a third volume to trace the conquest of the gospel into yet more of the Gentile world.

Luke could have sung Frederick W. Faber's hymn, "There's a wideness in God's mercy like the wideness of the sea."

HUMANITY

Some see significance in the position of Luke as the 42nd book in the Bible. Those interested in Bible numerics point out that 42 is the product of seven (the number of divine perfection) times six

---

1. *Addresses on Luke*, Loizeaux Brothers, 1947, p. 629.

(the number of man). Whether or not this numerical spot has meaning, Luke stresses that in the person of Jesus of Nazareth God became man. Luke bows before the great "mystery of godliness: God was manifested in the flesh" (1 Tim. 3:16).

Key phrase

In Luke Jesus calls Himself the "Son of Man" at least 24 times, linking the God of heaven with earth. This second Adam came to repair the damage caused by the fall of the first Adam, redeeming sinner and creation from the bondage of corruption.

Luke records instances where Jesus refers to Himself as the Son of Man, in which parallel passages omit this title. For example, "Blessed are ye, when men shall . . . reproach you, and cast out your name as evil, for the Son of man's sake" (6:22). But Matthew puts it, "Blessed are ye, when men shall . . . say all manner of evil against you falsely, for my sake" (5:11). See 12:8 and Matt. 10:32. Only in Luke do we have these statements in which Jesus terms Himself the Son of Man (17:22; 18:8; 21:36).

Birth and early life

Luke gives us the most complete coverage of Jesus' birth. Mary must have opened her heart to this warm-hearted physician. Wouldn't a physician have great interest in the story of a virgin birth? How reassuring that the chief testimony to this unique event comes from a doctor. Only Luke includes the details surrounding the unusual birth of Jesus' forerunner, John the Baptist. Only Luke tells of angel Gabriel's announcement to Mary, Mary's visit to Elizabeth, the Magnificat, the birth in the manger, the baby wrapped in swaddling clothes, the announcement of the angels to the shepherds in Bethlehem, and the visit of the shepherds who came seeking not a King, as did the wise men in Matthew's account, but rather a Savior, "Christ the Lord" (2:11).

Only Luke records His circumcision, presentation in the temple, adoration by Anna and Simeon, His visit at the age of 12 to the Temple where He surprised the rabbis with His questions and answers (the only event mentioned between His infancy and start of His public ministry), all in chapter 2. Only Luke mentions His age of 30 at His baptism (3:21-23).

I recall that my father kept records of my progress in school and in little league sports. Each birthday he stood me against a fencepost, measured my height, then made a notch to mark my progress. Luke tells us that Jesus, like any boy, grew "in wisdom and stature, and in favor with God and man" (2:52).

Links to human history

Luke is the Gospel author who links Jesus to human history. Only after careful investigation did he sit down and write his orderly account. His is the longest of the Gospels both in Greek and in English. (Check your New Testament to see that Luke's 24 chapters run longer than Matthew's 28). Scholars have found Luke to be a thorough researcher and painstaking historian, remarkably precise in his references to political offices and secular events. For example, he refers to the "decree from Caesar Augustus, that all the world should be taxed. (And this taxing was first made when Cyrenius was governor of Syria)" (2:1, 2).

Also, Luke places the start of John the Baptist's ministry "in the fifteenth year of the reign of Tiberias Ceasar, Pontius Pilate being governor of Judea, and Herod being tetrarch of Galilee, and his brother Philip tetrarch of Iturea and of the region of Trachonitis, and Lysanias the tetrarch of Abilene, Annas and Caiaphas being the high priests . . ." (3:1, 2).

In the opening chapters he records several time frames valuable to a historian. He writes "in the days of Herod" (1:5); "in the sixth month" (1:26); "about three months" (1:56); "And when eight days were accomplished" (2:21), "Anna . . . seven years . . . a widow of about fourscore and four years" (2:36, 37).

The Temptation episode

The temptation of our first parents to eat the forbidden fruit appealed to the lust of the flesh (good to eat), to the lust of the eyes (good to look on), and to the pride of life (would make them wise). The temptation of the second Adam made the same three appeals (Luke 4:1-13). Jesus, hungry, was asked to turn stones to bread (appeal to the flesh), was shown the kingdoms of this world (appeal to the eyes), and was invited to show off by jumping from the temple pinnacle (pride of life). The first Adam dragged the race down by yielding to these allurements. But the second Adam resisted the same types of temptation, and in the same sequence. Jesus was the perfect Man, victorious where Adam had failed. Note that the order of the temptations in Matthew reverses the second and third, making the offer of the kingdoms the climactic test, this in keeping with Matthew's emphasis on the kingship of Jesus.

Sermon on the Mount

Luke's setting for the Sermon on the Mount is significant. Whereas Matthew has Jesus going up into a mountain, a location fit for a king (5:11), Luke has Jesus coming down from the mountain to teach on a plateau (6:17). This lower level, though still among the mountain ranges, seems more suited to a man.

Later, Jesus crossed the Sea of Galilee in a storm. Though other Gospels mention Jesus already asleep in the boat, only Luke says He fell asleep, certainly a human proneness (8:23).

Slow journey toward Jerusalem

Here's a simple outline of Luke:

    I.   Preface - - - - - - - - - - - - - - - - - -1:1—4:44
   II. Birth and Childhood - - - - - - - - - -1:5—2:52
  III. Baptism, Genealogy, Temptation - -3:1—4:13
  IV. Ministry in Galilee - - - - - - - - - - -4:14—9:50
   V. Journey toward Jerusalem - - - - - - -9:51—19:28
  VI. Closing Ministry - - - - - - - - - - - -19:29—21:38
 VII. Death, Resurrection, Ascension - - -22:1—24:53

Luke is unique in recording Jesus' slow but progressive journey toward Jerusalem in a section covering about ten chapters (See V above). Note the repeated reference to Jerusalem as His destination (9:51; 13:22; 17:11; 18:31; 19:11, 28). This "Great Interpolation," as it is called, contains material not found in Matthew, Mark or John, including 17 parables, among them some of the most vivid, like the Good Samaritan (10:30-37), the rich fool (12:16-21), the prodigal son (15:11-32), the unjust steward (16:1-13), and the Pharisee and the publican (18:9-14).

At His passion

Only Luke records Jesus weeping over Jerusalem (19:41), and an angel coming to strengthen Him in Gethsemane (22:43).

Matthew and Mark record the centurion after the crucifixion calling Jesus "the Son of God" (Matt. 27:54; Mark 15:39). Luke reports the soldier's remark as, "Certainly this was a righteous man"

(23:47). The centurion doubtless made both statements, but each writer selected the one that suited his portrait.

Accent on common human practices

To pray is so human. Even non-Christians turn to prayer in times of desperation. To sing is also human. Luke is the Gospel of prayer and praise, so often spontaneous outlets of human emotion. Humor, also, is characteristic of humanity.

Prayer

Luke writes more about our Lord's practice of prayer than any other Gospel author. Over twenty times Jesus' praying is mentioned in the four Gospels, but over half are in Luke. Prayer was the habit of His life. A strong argument for the reality of prayer is the simple fact that the strong Son of God, Creator and Sustainer of the universe, found it necessary to pray. In His humanity He cried out for help and wisdom over and over. How much more do we frail humans need to do the same!

At every major crisis Jesus prayed: at His baptism (3:21); after healing a leper (5:16); all night before choosing the Twelve (6:12); before Peter's confession (9:18); at the Transfiguration (9:29); before teaching the Twelve how to pray (11:1); for Peter in the hour of his denial (22:32); in Gethsemane (22:39-46); His first and last cries from the cross (23:34, 46). Except for Gethsemane, all are exclusive to Luke.

Daniel S. Gregory says of our Lord's experience in Gethsemane, "While Matthew maintains his habits of careful grouping of events, and Mark his intense and vivid expressions, and both record the fact that Jesus went thrice from His disciples and repeated the prayer to His Father; Luke represents the whole as a season of prayer, connected with a great crisis in the spiritual experience of Jesus, in which the agony increased in power until it reached the intensest pitch" when His sweat became like great drops of blood. [2]

Three parables with lessons on prayer are found only in Luke: the friend at midnight (11:5-9), the unjust judge (18:1-8), and the Pharisee and the publican (18:9-14).

---

2. *Why Four Gospels?*, Bible League Book Co., Bible House, New York, 1907, p. 255.

Praise

Only in Luke do we have five songs associated with Jesus' birth: Elisabeth's Song (1:41-45), Mary's Magnificat (1:46-55), Zacharias' Psalm (1:67-79), the Angels' Song to the shepherds (2:8-14), and Simeon's Song (*Nunc Dimittis*) (2:28-32). Though not given the contents of her praise, we are told that the prophetess Anna also gave thanks in the Temple (2:36-38). One tradition claims that Luke was a poet as well as a doctor. A characteristic word in Luke is *glorify*— ascribing praise to God. Among those extolling God were shepherds (2:20), synagogue attendants (4:15), the healed paralytic and those seeing the miracle (5:25, 26), those witnessing the raising of the widow of Nain's son (7:16), the crippled woman healed (13:13), the healed leper (17:15), blind Bartimaeus when he regained his sight (18:43), the centurion in charge of the crucifixion (23:47).

Luke likes to speak of joyous occasions. He opens with the angel Gabriel bringing glad tidings to Zacharias about the birth of his son (1:19). Later he states that the angels of heaven rejoice when a sinner repents (15:7, 10). The last verse of his Gospel reports that Jesus' disciples returned to Jerusalem after the Ascension, and "were continually in the temple, praising and blessing God." The use of *sunchairein*, meaning to "rejoice together," is exclusively Lukan.

Humor

Dr. Tenney says, "Another device which appears in Luke's homiletical practice is the use of humor. His humor is not buffoonery or shallow burlesque. . . . He has a happy disposition and often sees the lighter side of life. In the parable of the great supper (Luke 14:15-24), he described the guests who sought to decline the invitation by using shallow excuses. The triviality of these seems ridiculous. The man who had bought a field did not seem to realize that if he had not seen the field before the purchase, he might have been badly cheated. The man who had purchased oxen without trying them was still more foolish. The man who had married a wife, and therefore could not come was most foolish of all. The law did excuse a bridegroom from military service (Deut. 24:5), but a banquet could hardly be classed as a war! The flimsiness of these excuses, offered as a concerted response to the invitation of the host, smacks of comedy, even though the parable is serious in its teaching." [3]

---

3. *The Genius of the Gospels*, Eerdmans, 1951, pp. 84, 85.

Jesus' post-resurrection appearance to the Emmaus disciples had its lighter side. Joining their conversation on recent events, Jesus asked what they were talking about and why so sad. The Expositor's Greek Testament comments, "The question of the stranger quietly put to the two wayfarers is not without a touch of humor." The very subject they had been discussing stands before them, and they fail to recognize Him. Moreover, He walks miles with them, teaching in His masterly way, still unrecognized till He finally reveals Himself (24:13-35). G. Campbell Morgan remarks, "There is a tender and beautiful playfulness in the way He dealt with these men. Humor is as divine as Pathos, and I cannot study the life of Jesus without finding humor there." [4]

COMPASSION

Norman Cousins said that over the door of every medical building should be written the word, "Compassion." Luke's observant and sympathetic medical interest shows through in his selection of details. For example, though three Gospels record the healing of the man with the withered hand, only Dr. Luke identifies it as the right hand (6:6). Only Dr. Luke recounts the healing of the woman severely crippled for eighteen years (13:11-17). Only Luke tells of Jesus' sweat as drops of blood (22:44). Though all Gospels tell of the wounding of Malchus' ear, only Dr. Luke reports its healing (22:51).

Only Luke notes Jesus' declaring His mission of sympathy for all classes of the needy: to preach good tidings to the poor, to proclaim release to captives, to heal the brokenhearted, the recovery of sight to the blind, and to set at liberty those bruised (4:18). The Great Physician reached out in mercy to the social outcast, the disenfranchised, the sick, and the sinful.

The despised Samaritans

The Jews considered the Samaritans half-breeds, and would have no dealings with them (John 4:9), so avoided traveling through Samaria. Jesus' enemies insultingly called Him "a Samaritan" (John 8:48). Though Matthew mentions Jesus' order to the Twelve not to enter "any city of the Samaritans" (10:5), Luke omits this prohibition. Rather, he tells how Jesus on His final journey to Jerusalem sent messengers ahead

---

4. *The Gospel According to Luke*, New York: Revell, 1931, p. 277.

into a Samaritan village to prepare them for His visit. Though the Samaritans rejected Him, Luke recounts that Jesus would not let James and John call down fire from heaven on the Samaritans (9:52-56).

Luke seems to go out of his way to report favorably on this despised race. For example, he portrays a Samaritan as a model of neighborliness in the parable of the Good Samaritan. In the story of only one of ten healed lepers returning to say thanks to Jesus, Luke adds, "and he was a Samaritan" (17:16).

Womanhood

Women held an inferior place in Jesus' day. Every morning a devout Jewish male recited a prayer in which he thanked God for not making "him a Gentile, a slave, or a woman." Luke highlights Jesus' frequent mention and elevation of womanhood.

The birth story is from Mary's vantage point, whereas Matthew sees it from Joseph's side. The narratives involving Elisabeth and Anna are found only in Luke (1 & 2).

Only Luke tells of the widow of Nain whom Jesus met on her way to bury her son. Luke underscores the deep sympathy Jesus had for this bereft widow. Telling her to "weep not," He raised the youth from death and restored him to his mother (7:11-15).

Luke alone tells of the sinner-woman who washed Jesus' feet with her tears and wiped them with her hair (7:36ff).

Jesus' ministry was partially supported by the gifts of "certain women, which had been healed of evil spirits and infirmities, Mary called Magdalene, out of whom went seven devils, and Joanna the wife of Chuza, Herod's steward, and Susanna, and many others, which ministered unto Him of their substance" (8:2, 3). Mention of this loyal band of female supporters, only by Luke, enhances the dignity of womanhood.

Only Luke tells of Jesus' visit to two sisters in Bethany, where He scolded Martha for over-concern of culinary preparation, and commended Mary for her desire to learn (10:38-42).

Luke alone tells of the woman with the spirit of infirmity (13:10ff), of the parable of the woman and her lost coin (15:8ff), of the parable of the widow and the unjust judge (18:1ff), and of the women who lamented Jesus on His way to the cross whom He addressed as "Daughters of Jerusalem" (23:27-31).

Only Luke tells of the faithful group of women who returned to their homes, after watching Jesus' burial, to prepare "spices and ointments, and rested the sabbath day," intending to give Jesus' body a proper anointing early Sunday (23:55, 56).

Bereaved, busy, burdened, broken women Jesus comforted, instructed, relieved, restored. In an age when a woman counted for little, mainly to please her husband, bear his children, and slave in his home, Jesus honored womanhood.

The home

Broken homes are common today. Dr. Luke knew the value of wholesome homes. Luke has been called "The Gospel of the Home" because of Jesus' home visits. Besides visits recorded in other Gospels, Luke alone tells of His eating meat in the house of Pharisee Simon (7:36-50); of hospitality in the home of Mary and Martha (10:38-42); of His words in the home of a chief Pharisee (14:1-14); of His inviting Himself to dinner in Zacchaeus' house (19:1-10); and of His eating in the Emmaus home (24:30-32).

Then His parables include the interruption of sleep in a home caused by the midnight arrival of a neighbor's friend (11:5-8); the woman searching her house for a lost coin (15:8-10); and the banquet at the prodigal's return (15:11-32).

When visiting Australia in 1990 I saw a newspaper article which told of a Christian group which ordered its followers to disown any family member who would not accept the Christian faith. Husbands and wives were to leave their mates. Children were to take what they could from their parents and leave home. Grandparents were given the ultimatum—become Christians or you won't see your grandchildren. How far from the heart of Jesus. Though the acceptance of Christ may cause division in a family, believers are exhorted to love unsaved family members, and to do all in their power to create peace and unity within the home.

Only child

We always feel extra sad when a child is sick. But when that child is an only child, it heightens the human pathos. On three occasions Luke speaks of the restoration of an only child. When Jesus stopped the funeral procession whose chief mourner was the widow of Nain, and brought her boy back to life, Luke wrote that he was "the only son of his mother" (7:12, 13).

Though Matthew, Mark and Luke relate the raising of Jairus' daughter, only Luke mentions she was an only daughter (8:42).

Also Luke tells of the healing of a demented boy whose father besought Jesus, "Look upon my son, for he is mine only child" (9:38). But Matthew omits this poignant fact.

The poor and disabled

In a resolution at its 1989 convention the National Association of Evangelicals, aware that thirty-five million Americans are classified as physically or mentally disabled, noted that disabled persons often experience unemployment, poverty, substance abuse, and depression. Evangelicals, therefore, recognizing that Jesus' ministry on earth singled out the weak, the poor and the disabled for special concern, "should reach out to disabled people with respect, acceptance into the life of the church, and special assistance." They should remove physical and communication barriers, offer transportation, and incorporate their gifts into the life of the church.

Perhaps because of His own childhood poverty Jesus had a soft spot in His heart for the poor and needy. Only Luke records that the offering Joseph and Mary brought at their baby's presentation in the temple was not the more costly present of a lamb, but instead the alternative permissible for the poor, a pair of doves or pigeons (2:22-24). This act shows the deep destitution of Jesus' parents who likely would never have furnished the lesser gift had the richer offering been within their means. It is thought that Joseph died some time before Jesus began His ministry. Was it seeing Mary's difficult life those many years that led Jesus to speak with concern for widows?

Luke is the only Gospel to spell out what John the Baptist meant by repentance. Among other things, it involved giving an extra coat to the coatless, food to the hungry, and avoiding violence and overcharging (3:10-14). The Baptist was a genuine forerunner in his aversion to poverty and oppression.

Only Luke gives the parable of the rich fool in which Jesus warns against filling up earthly barns while neglecting to deposit treasure in the bank of heaven (12:13-21). A major method of laying up heavenly treasure is helping the poor.

Luke alone relates the story of the rich man and Lazarus in which Jesus' sympathy clearly rests with Lazarus who, sick with sores and reduced to beggary, proves to be far better off in the next world. There, with tables reversed, the rich man becomes a poor beggar, pleading for a single drop of water (16:19-31).

The sinful

The Greeks were looking for the perfect man. Realizing their own imperfection, they tended to find the cause of their shortcoming in human limitation. Luke wanted to make it clear that the root culprit was sin, and aimed to arouse in his readers a sense of their own sinfulness. So he painted sin as sin and clearly condemned it. When someone in a crowd asked Jesus to intervene with his brother to share the inheritance, Jesus warned him against covetousness. Luke frequently employed the term "lost" to show the need of being saved. Luke uses the word "sinner" oftener than all the other Gospel writers combined.

Then, more than any other Gospel writer, Luke emphasizes the willingness of Jesus to welcome and forgive sinners. It is Luke who tells us that Jesus, when a guest in the home of Simon the Pharisee, permitted a "woman in the city, which was a sinner" to wash, wipe, repeatedly kiss and anoint His feet. When the Pharisee complained at Jesus' action, Jesus countered, "Her sins, which are many, are forgiven; for she loved much; but to whom little is forgiven, the same loveth little" (7:36-50).

When a crowd of tax-collectors, considered the scum of society, drew near to hear Jesus, the Pharisees murmured, "This man receiveth sinners" (15:1, 2). In response Jesus gave three parables, all peculiar to Luke and involving lost things: the lost sheep, the lost coin, and the prodigal son. Heaven rejoices at the finding of the lost! But the elder son, who sulked into the night at the fatherly welcome given his prodigal brother, reflected the insensitivity of the Pharisees toward repentant sinners. How out of tune were those religionists with heaven.

Luke alone tells of the two men who went up to the temple to pray. The Pharisee's prayer was really a listing of his good deeds in an attempt to merit divine favor. But the publican with bowed head begged, "God, be merciful to me a sinner." Jesus' evaluation—it was the man who admitted his sinful condition who returned to his home justified in God's sight.

Only Luke carries the conversion of Zacchaeus, rich director of Jericho's IRS. When Jesus invited Himself to Zacchaeus' home, the crowd murmured, "That He was gone to be a guest with a man that is a sinner" (19:7). Jesus' answer summarizes both the story of Zacchaeus and the book of Luke, "For the Son of man is come to seek and to save that which is lost" (19:10).

Only Luke tells of the repentant thief (23:42, 43).

Luke features the sympathy of Jesus for the lost, the last, the least and the lowest. Available and approachable today, the Savior still calls the dropout, the misfit, the reject, the prostitute, the drug-addict, the prisoner, the AIDS victim.

Jesus can take cinders, clinkers, and hopeless lives, and make them gloriously new. He can transform ashes into diamonds. Someone quipped, "Jesus can turn an eyesore into a sight for sore eyes."

A man, browsing among the weather-beaten tombstones of an old English graveyard, came across an inscription that had been kept clean and legible. It read, "He was compassionate." Whoever this long-dead stranger might have been, he had the kind of heart God wants us to cultivate in the midst of our cruel and callous world.

8

It's Tough to Be Tender

W hen Erich Honecker, 77-year-old-East German Communist leader, was ousted in October 1989 with no place to go, he and his wife were given shelter in two tiny guest rooms in a Protestant pastor's home in Lobetal, a village devoted to caring for the mentally handicapped and elderly. Many East Germans were outraged at the pastor for lodging Honecker because of his luxurious lifestyle, hardline regime, and persecution of church-based dissidents which, among other hardships, had prevented the pastor's own children from entering university. But the clergymen of Lobetal said they considered it their Christian duty to shelter Honecker despite his Stalinist rule of East Germany for two decades, explaining, "We could hardly have a welcoming statue of Jesus Christ in the village, then leave someone outside the door who has gotten into trouble." For 85 years the 1200-place Lobetal (Valley of Praise) center, a group of cottages and clinics set in the woods, has looked after the weak. "The once-powerful Honecker is now one of the weak," commented the pastors. He was recovering from cancer surgery.

The Christian church has a history of tenderness from its beginning. When first-century persecution thrust them into the public stadiums to be torn to pieces by wild beasts, the strong always protected the weak, right to the very end. The strong had learned compassionate behavior from their Master. After reading the entire Gospel of Luke for the first time, a young lady exclaimed, "Wow! Like Jesus has this totally intense thing for ragamuffins!" Jesus seems to have spent a large slice of His time with the down-and-outers, the immoral, the unlovely and unloved, the least and last. He related to them with warmth and tenderness, and wishes His followers to do the same.

But it's not always easy to be tender. Despite widespread acts of heroism like the rescue of a drowning person, the brave thwarting of a crime, or the dangerous digging of a shaft to save a miner, the world is basically unsympathetic. Cruelty lurks close to the surface of civilization. The milk of human kindness is in short supply. Much of mankind is callous, indifferent to others in distress. One little roughneck boasted how tough he was, "On my street, the farther out you go, the tougher they get, and I live in the last house."

Even church members often lack sympathetic understanding. Enjoying good health and prosperous times, and hearing of Christian brothers and sisters in need, some shrug it off with a casual, "Too bad; everyone has his troubles," or "Why don't they get out and earn their way, like the rest of us?" People laid aside are soon forgotten—no one comes to visit. One man spoke of "the lost chord of sympathy."

Press, radio, and TV bring the world and its staggering weight of woes right into our living room. The constant bombardment of famines, earthquakes, wars, storms, accidents, muggings, rapes, and murders ceases to boggle the mind. Emotionally jaded, we often wrap ourselves in our own little world of interests and fail to extend a needed, helping hand.

Against this backdrop of unconcern stands the command of Scripture to be tenderhearted. An unmerciful spirit is inconsistent with the love of God. What we need are skins as thick as an elephant, and hearts as tender as a dove. We need a thick epidermis to absorb the barbs and blows aimed at us, and a sensitive heart to weep with those who weep.

Christianity is more than merely abstinence from certain practices, or the ritualistic attendance at church plus private devotions and giving to missions. True faith proves its love for our fellowmen by deeds to alleviate their sufferings. The biblical message flashes: "Wanted—Tender Hearts." Paul wrote, "Clothe yourselves with compassion" (Col. 3:12 NIV). But *IT'S TOUGH TO BE TENDER.* How do we cultivate a compassionate heart?

REMEMBER—WE HAVE A TENDER GOD

Compassion is a fundamental and distinctive quality of the biblical conception of *God, the Father.* He revealed Himself to Moses in Mt. Sinai as "the compassionate and gracious God, slow to anger, abounding in love" (Ex. 34:6). The lamenting Jeremiah declared, "It is of the Lord's mercies that we are not consumed, because His compassions fail not. They are new every morning" (Lam. 3:22, 23). Mercy was a quality required of the Old Testament community. Jesus taught, "Be merciful, just as your Father is merciful" (Lk. 6:36 NIV). The compassion of the earthly father toward his prodigal son reflects the heavenly Father's mercy toward His wayward children.

Repeatedly it was said that *God, the Son* was "moved with compassion" over pitiable people: the hungry (Matt. 15:32; Mk. 6:34; 8:2), a man with a withered hand (Matt. 14:14), the blind (Matt. 20:34), lepers (Mk. 1:41), demon-possessed (Mk. 5:19; 9:22), the sorrowing (Lk. 7:13), and the shepherdless (Matt. 9:36). Commending the compassion of the Good Samaritan toward an alien victim (Lk. 10:33), Jesus taught us to extend kindness to anyone in need crossing our path, enemy as well as friend.

God, the Holy Spirit descended as a dove at the baptism of Jesus. The dove is a gentle, sensitive bird, symbolic of the tender Holy Spirit, so easily grieved by a believer's unkind conduct (Eph. 4:30-32).

IDENTIFY WITH THE DOWNTRODDEN

A seminary class was studying Luke 4:16-19, which tells of Jesus' reading in his hometown synagogue the Scripture from Isaiah about the Spirit anointing Him to preach good news to the poor, to proclaim freedom for prisoners, recovery of sight for the blind, and release for the oppressed. The teacher asked, "What role do you identify with?" The white men in the class responded, "The preacher." But the women and minority men answered, "The poor, the prisoners, the blind, and the oppressed." Though preachers are to proclaim good news, they also share responsibility to identify with the downtrodden.

The incarnation of Jesus was the ultimate of God's compassion fleshed out in action. So thoroughly did Jesus identify Himself with us that He took the punishment that won our forgiveness upon Him on the cross. During His ministry Jesus offered one-to-one, hands-on mercy, not refusing those who supposedly brought their sad condition on themselves. He took the initiative, accepted the scorned as friends and equals, and gave them a sense of dignity by liberating them from their captivity. He took their troubles on Himself, even to the point of tears. A Britisher recalls two newspaper pictures of King George VI of England. The first showed him at his coronation with his ermine robes, jeweled crown, in the midst of impressive pomp. The second showed him in a section of London which had been bombed into rubble by the Nazis, inspecting the damage along with Winston Churchill. He wore no ermine nor crown, looking remarkably common. But as he walked through the debris, he wept. Churchill records in his memoirs that as the people saw their king weeping midst their ruin, they kept repeating, "He loves us." Jesus, Lord of glory, laid aside His outer splendor, became one with us, walked our vale of tears, and weeps with us.

We cannot evade responsibility for compassion by busyness in ministry, claiming that others will have to care for the mercy side of things. A major lesson in the parable of the Good Samaritan is the preoccupation of the priest and Levite with their own religious duties which blinded them to the plight of the victim in their path. We cannot tarry too long on the Mt. of Transfiguration lest we miss the agonizing cries at our doorstep. All around us are suffering folks, a grieving mother, a severely depressed neighbor, a pain-racked friend, a discriminated-against associate, a fellow-employee feeling a broken relationship. We must identify the sufferers in our midst, and make their pain our pain. What can help us take their pain into our hearts?

Imagination

Compassion can be stimulated by use of our imagination. Abraham Lincoln once said, "I am sorry for the man who can't feel the whip when it is laid on another man's back." Compassion means to "feel with." Let the healthy wonder what life is like to those confined to the four walls of a hospital, or to a wheelchair. Let the mature imagine how it feels to be young with the youth's fears and temptations. Let the youth picture what it means to be old and frail.

Let the well-to-do wonder what poverty must be like. And let those with normal IQs put themselves in the shoes of a mentally retarded person.

The summer after his sophomore year a 19-year-old college student worked as a cub reporter at his hometown newspaper. A traveling group of young, enthusiastic, aspiring actors were working on four plays to present later on. They were also altering a broken-down store into a theater. The theater manager worriedly commented, "It's a lot for them to get ready."

Though the regular critic was covering the play, the cub reporter decided to attend opening night and write a review just for the editor's eyes. Perhaps he would run it, if written with enough sting. So, with salty phrases he noted that most of the actors were his own age, that they were all jittery, that the female lead fumbled her opening line, and that her male counterpart entered from the wrong door. Though he did cleverly ad-lib a few lines that covered this error, the reporter didn't bother to jot that down.

After the play and a standing ovation, the regular critic remarked about the enthusiasm of the actors, but the cub reporter didn't respond, for he was dreaming about the sharp sentences he was planning to write. He worked late to polish it off, handed it to the editor who first glanced over the piece, then gave it his undivided attention. Laughing out loud, the editor remarked, "This is funny. I'm going to run this review too."

Next day the cub reporter met the theater manager downtown and, intoxicated with self-satisfaction over his well-crafted critique, asked him how he liked his review. The manager's words struck like a sword, "You hurt a lot of people." The cub reporter, wishing to win applause, had not realized how his biting criticisms would make those actors feel. The manager said softly, "You write well. But don't forget—all work is difficult, and life is too. Instead of using our talents to tear down so we'll look smart, wouldn't we better try to help each other become excellent?" The reporter never forgot this advice. From then on he imagined himself in the shoes of those he critiqued, and wrote only with positive outlook. [1]

---

1. *Reader's Digest*, "The Best Criticism I Ever Received," July 1986, pp. 134-136.

Experience

Experience may teach us compassion. God told Israel to be kind to strangers for they themselves were once strangers in Egypt. Suffering should mellow and mold us into ministers of compassion. During Queen Victoria's reign, she heard of a commoner's wife who had lost her baby. Having experienced the same sorrow herself, the queen decided to visit the mother. So she spent some time with her. Afterwards her neighbors asked what the queen said. "Nothing," replied the grieving mother. "She simply put her hands on mine, and we wept together."

Mary Reed, born in America in 1858, went as a missionary to India. Broken in health after eight years of work, she was sent to the Himalayan foothills to rest. For the first time she observed a community of 500 lepers, abandoned and without human help or comfort. Returning to her station, she was always haunted by the pitiful sight of those lepers. She worked for another year, but her health so collapsed that she was sent home to America where her case baffled the doctors. One day she felt a tingling sensation in the forefinger of her right hand, and noticed a strange spot on her cheek. It dawned on her what was wrong—she was a leper. She was sent to a specialist in New York City who confirmed her suspicion. Without telling her mother, she headed back to India, and straight to the leper settlement she had seen five years before. Writing her mother about her illness, she said, "I shall have the joy of ministering to a class of people who but for me would have no missionary at all."

At her first meeting with the lepers she told them, "I have been called by God to come and help you." Tears ran down their cheeks as they thought of the suffering in store for their new friend. She plunged into a busy life, ministering and teaching, despite the rapid progress of the disease. When the illness was somewhat arrested, she attended a conference for missionaries in India. Called to the front to give a scheduled address, she felt unequal to the task because of her hoarse throat, and could only whisper, "Let us sing." Whereupon the crowd sang, "O, for a thousand tongues to sing our great Redeemer's praise." She started a hospital which gave lepers not only new bodies but renewed souls. Altogether she labored over 40 years as superintendent of that settlement in the Himalayas. Her experience with the lepers from the very first contact had motivated her to a mission of touching untouchables.

Potential

In a third-century debate on Christianity, heathen Celsus said to church father Origen, "When most teachers go forth to teach, they cry, 'Come to me, you who are clean and worthy,' and they are followed by the highest caliber of people available. But your silly master cries, 'Come to me, you who are down and beaten by life,' and so he accumulates around him the rag, tag and bobtail of humanity."

Origen replied, "Yes, they are the rag, tag and bobtail of humanity. But Jesus does not leave them that way. Out of material you would have thrown away as useless, he fashions men, giving them back their self-respect, enabling them to stand on their feet and look God in the eyes. They were cowed, cringing, broken things. But the Son has set them free."

The Twelve whom Jesus called to be His disciples were a group who would never have been voted "most likely to succeed." Philip seemed indecisive. Thomas displayed cynicism. Zealot Simon was a revolutionary. Simon was unstable. James and John were status-hungry and fiercely intolerant. Matthew was a despised tax-collector. But Jesus looked on each one with compassion and was so patient in teaching them. When their exceptional training was anointed with the Holy Spirit at Pentecost, this nondescript, ragtag, dullish, fearful, impulsive, fiery, unlettered gang of throne-climbers and deserters were transformed into a revitalized, united, godly band of bold and loving evangelists, purged from much of their pride, anger, ambition, impatience, instability, cheating, and vindictiveness.

Jesus saw these men, not only as they were, but as they could become. As we look at the fallen and despised, we need to focus the eye of faith on their potential. Charles Colson, who spent time in prison because of his involvement in Watergate, developed enormous sympathy for those in jail, not only because of his own incarceration in the penal system, but also because he knew that these men could become upstanding, law-abiding, productive citizens. So he founded Prison Fellowship, a ministry that has reached into over 100 American prisons. In one recent year, 70 week-long "In-Prison Seminars" were held in 40 states and 30 federal institutions. Several hundred inmates have graduated from his Washington Seminar program which involves furloughed federal inmates spending two weeks of intensive Bible study and discipleship training in the nation's capital. The author of Hebrews thanked his readers because they "had compassion on the prisoners" (10:34 RSV).

PERSONALLY ACT TO HELP SOME NEARBY NEEDY

An article in the Medicine section of *Newsweek* tells how doctors are learning sensitivity along with anatomy. Several medical colleges now have programs to make sure that the compassion and humanity students bring to school is not lost. Not only doctors, but all who follow the Great Physician need soft, sympathetic hearts (August 12, 1991).

The director of a Pennsylvania organization targeting youth in need, sent out a card with this probing monologue.

"I was hungry and you formed a humanities club to discuss my hunger. Thank you.

"I was imprisoned and you crept off guiltily to your chapel in the cellar and prayed for my release.

"I was naked and in your mind you debated the morality of my appearance.

"I was sick and you knelt and thanked God for your health.

"I was homeless and you preached to me of the spiritual shelter of the love of God.

"I was lonely and you left me alone to pray for me. You seem so holy, so close to God. But I am still very hungry and lonely and cold.

"By the grace of almighty God and the gift of compassion, please help us reach the hungry—the lonely—those who are cold physically and spiritually." [2]

A group of Christian college students enjoyed their weekly discussion of fine doctrinal points. Halfway through the semester it dawned on them that they were not practicing their faith. They said, "Let's do something." They began to put feet to their doctrine. They called it the "Just do it" principle.

When Jesus told His hearers to love their neighbor, they tried to beg the question by asking, "Who is my neighbor?" It was then that He gave the parable of the Good Samaritan, which so pointedly teaches that our neighbor is anyone in need who crosses our path,

2. Bill Drury, Teen Haven, PO Box 31, Willow Street, PA, 17584.

regardless of race or status. If we see a brother in need, and fail to help, how dwells the love of God in us? (1 Jn. 3:17). Every time that Jesus was moved with compassion, He acted to alleviate misery.

Compassion has launched many secular crusades. *Newsweek* reported the success of a plan to bus part of Boston's overflowing homeless population to the suburbs at night during the winter of 1988. At first, some of the 38,000 residents of Braintree, a middle-class suburb 15 miles to the south chosen as the first nighttime shelter, cried "not in my backyard." They feared the influx of drug abusers and deinstitutionalized mentally ill would make their suburb a magnet for Boston's 3,500 homeless. But when the plan went into effect in November, the people's fear gave way to compassion. Neighbors began to donate clothes and volunteers to serve meals at the temporary dormitory in a state-owned armory. High-school students contributed $1,000. Cub scouts brought cookies. Women knitted 25 woolen hats. Police reported no major disorders (3/6/89, p. 27).

The Salvation Army started a program so the homeless of New York city could secure a high-school equivalent diploma (GED). Transforming the basement of their Manhattan Central Citadel Corps into a dormitory, the Army recruited its first students from the cavernous confines of Grand Central Station. Given free lodging, they agreed to a strict code of conduct. The graduation service for the 13 who successfully completed its first course, the class of May '87, was held in the terminal of Grand Central station, where they once lived. As curious commuters looked on, the ten men and three women marched one by one to receive their diplomas. Some, evicted from their apartments after loss of jobs, had lived in the streets, the subways, and in Grand Central Station for years. Four of the class were accepted at Fordham University for the fall. Some dubbed their graduation, "Pomp and Better Circumstances." Jesus, Who had nowhere to lay His head, rejoices when the homeless receive shelter.

Many compassionate individuals have initiated support groups to minister to the troubled: unwed mothers, abused women, prisoners, orphans, singles, divorced, bereaved, unemployed, alcoholics, drug addicts, AIDS victims, and the hungry, to name a few. *World Vision* magazine told of a retired gold miner with a nose for hidden treasure. In a seven-year period he dug up $118,000 worth of help for the poor, all from a dumpster behind a local supermarket. He advises that, since the store's management cannot officially grant permission, just start showing up at the back of the store and start picking out usable items from the garbage. Also, keep the area tidy, tell any store employee that the food is going to the needy, and establish a network of distribution, like a rescue mission or church food cupboards.

Hospices provide a ministry to the terminally ill. After all, in western Europe at least, it was the church reaching out to the sick and the suffering, which founded hospitals. The tradition has been carried on through medical missionaries who have started clinics and dispensed medicine to those who might otherwise have never seen a doctor in their lifetime. How vividly I recall driving into an African village and seeing a little boy lying motionless on the ground. Our driver, a doctor, stepped from the jeep to examine the boy. "Malaria," he said. Later that evening, after returning to a missionary's residence to get medicine, we drove back to the pitch blackness of that village, where the doctor handed the boy's father the medicine. The doctor compassionately remarked, "Now the boy will live."

Many times our compassion will have to be directed toward members of our own family. A poignant article in *Christianity Today*, written by Dr. Robert McQuilkin, president of Columbia Bible College and Seminary, tells of his struggle between two callings upon learning that his wife had Alzheimer's disease. To which commitment should he be loyal: his marriage vows or his school presidency? When her condition worsened, the school board arranged for a companion to stay in her home during the day so he could go to the office. But it became impossible to keep Muriel home. Soon after he left, and distressed without him, she would take out after him. The walk to school and back was a mile. Some days she made the trip ten times. At night, when he helped her off with her shoes, he found bloody feet. When he told their family doctor, he choked up, and simply said, "Such love."

As she required more and more of him, he wrestled with the question of who would get him full-time—Muriel or Columbia Bible College and Seminary? She had cared for him almost 40 years with utmost devotion. If he took care of her the next 40, he knew he would still be in her debt. But how could he walk away from a ministry so challenging and signally blessed for 22 years? After months of agonizing reflection and prayer, he decided that the school did not need a part-time, distracted president. In the best interests of both his loves, school and wife, he resigned. The school has since named him chancellor, a position which benefits from his expertise, yet permits him to care for his wife. His decision has caused many husbands and wives to renew their wedding vows, and act and react with more compassion toward their mates. [3]

DEPEND ON THE SOURCE OF COMPASSION

To stir up compassion we must first realize that we have been the recipients of God's magnanimous tenderness. In the parable of the unmerciful servant Jesus taught that the servant who had been forgiven much should have had pity on his fellowservant who owed him so little (Matt. 18:23-35). Through the Cross God has forgiven us all our many sins. Comprehending the enormity of the debt God has forgiven us should awaken compassion in our hearts for others. As Paul summed it up, "Be ye kind one to another, tenderhearted, forgiving one another, even as God for Christ's sake hath forgiven you" (Eph. 4:32).

To maintain a tender attitude we need the help of the Holy Spirit. Is He not called the Comforter Who not only comforts us but comforts others through us? The dove in its tenderness is a symbol of the Holy Spirit. Jesus was the epitome of tenderness, so often moved with compassion toward those in distressing circumstances. How significant that Luke mentions the close connection of the Holy Spirit with events in Jesus' life, showing that the Holy Spirit was the source of His tenderheartedness.

The angel Gabriel explained the miraculous conception to the Virgin Mary, "The Holy Ghost shall come upon thee" (1:35).

Elizabeth, visited by the Virgin Mary, and "filled with the Holy Ghost" blessed her as "the mother of my Lord" (1:41-43).

In Simeon's blessing of the infant Jesus in the Temple, the Holy Spirit is mentioned three times (2:25-27).

When Jesus was baptized, "the Holy Ghost descended in a bodily shape like a dove upon Him" (3:22).

Jesus returned from Jordan "full of the Holy Ghost," and "was led by the Spirit into the wilderness" for His temptation (4:1). After His victory over temptation Jesus returned in the power of the Spirit into Galilee to begin His ministry (4:14).

No other Gospel approximates Luke in emphasizing the Holy

---

3. "Living by Vows," October 8, 1990, pp. 38-40.

Spirit's involvement at the start of Jesus' life. Luke also says that, as Jesus began His ministry in His hometown synagogue at Nazareth, He read publicly the Scripture, "The Spirit of the Lord is upon Me, because He hath anointed Me to preach . . ." (4:18).

In the middle of His ministry we learn that Jesus was "full of joy through the Holy Spirit" (10:21). Though Matthew says that our heavenly Father will give good things to those who ask Him, Luke's parallel passage singles out the Holy Spirit as the gift which the Father will give (Matt. 7:7; Luke 11:13).

At His ascension, Jesus told His disciples to wait in Jerusalem until "endued with power from on high" (24:29), meaning until the Holy Spirit came upon them at Pentecost.

An old man carried a little can of oil everywhere. If he passed a door that squeaked, he put a little oil on the hinges. If a gate did not open easily, he oiled the latch. Passing through life, he lubricated the hard places, making it easier for others. Though thought eccentric, he plodded on, refilling his can of oil. The Lord Jesus used the oil of the Spirit to make life smoother for the downed and despised. Around us many lives creak and grate harshly day by day. Though it's tough to be tender, we need to be available with the oil of the Spirit.

9

Uniquely in John

A high-school teacher, known for his non-Christian bias, was visibly rankled when a senior in classroom discussion calmly affirmed his belief in the Bible as the Word of God. The teacher decided to embarrass the Christian boy for his "outmoded" view. So the teacher suggested a debate, "Resolved that the Bible is the Word of God," asking the Christian to take the affirmative. He was careful to choose for the negative a boy who was both the brightest student and best debater in the class.

As the day for the debate arrived, the teacher inwardly gloated over how his star pupil would make mincemeat out of his opponent. His anticipation was reinforced when the Christian lad, surprisingly, did not present an orderly argument, but merely quoted a few verses from the Bible, commenting confidently that the Word of God was fully able to defend itself.

The teacher could scarcely contain himself as he called on his bright student who, instead of offering a demolishing rebuttal, made this confession. "I never read much of the Bible before. So I thought that to debate the question intelligently, I should read at least a part of it. I chose the Gospel of John, and have read it through, not once, but five times. Not only have I come to believe that the Bible is the Word of God, but I've also come to believe that Jesus is the Son of God. And I now trust Him as my Savior!" The story ends with a shocked and angry teacher dismissing a bemused class.

The Gospel of John may have led more people to faith in Christ than any other book in the Bible, or out of it. This fits John's avowed evangelistic purpose, "These are written, that ye might believe that Jesus is the Christ, the Son of God; and that believing ye might have life through His name" (20:31). This book contains the Bible's best known verse—John 3:16—often called the "gospel in a nutshell." The Gideon Bible in its opening comments prints John 3:16 in 22 languages.

Words which characterize John's Gospel are deity, simplicity, sevens, Father-related, and belief.

DEITY

Cerinthus, a first-century heretic, taught that Jesus was merely human, the son of Joseph and Mary by natural descent. Tradition says that one day John, on his way to bathe at Ephesus, spotted Cerinthus at the bathhouse, and fled without bathing, shouting, "Let us flee, lest even the bathhouse fall down because the enemy of the truth, Cerinthus, is within." Perhaps John wrote this gospel to offset Cerinthus' heresy by proving that Jesus was God.

John gives the loftiest view of Jesus

Whereas Matthew, Mark, and Luke view Jesus mainly through historical narrative, John fixes our attention on His majesty through selected miracles, discourses, claims and conversations.

Jesus is recognized as divine from the very beginning. Every chapter in some way displays His deity, either through a title, "Son of God" (1:49), or through a miracle like turning water into wine (2:1-11), or through an attribute like omniscience (4:18) or preexistence (8:58), or through a claim to some prerogative of deity like both raising and judging the dead (5:22, 28, 29), or through the reception of worship reserved only for deity (20:28).

If Matthew, Mark, and Luke lead us into the Holy Place, John takes us beyond into the Holy of Holies. In John Jesus is certainly King (1:49), Servant (13:1-17), and Son of Man (4:7; 11:35). But He is pre-eminently the eternal Son of God Who dwelt in the bosom of the Father, came down to earth, lived among men, then returned to His heavenly home. Here's a short outline, based on 16:28.

I. "I came forth from the Father" (Prologue)   1: 1-18
II. "And am come into the world" (Ministry)   1:19-12:50
III. "Again, I leave the world" (Short period in Upper
Room and walk to Garden)   13 -17
IV. "And go to the Father" (Arrest, Cross, Burial, Resurrection)   18 -21

John's fitness to write this lofty Gospel

It's not surprising that John gave us an exalted portrait of Jesus. He belonged to Jesus' inner circle of three. He was positioned next to Jesus at the Last Supper, earning him the title in the early church "The Epistethios"—the one who reclined on Jesus' bosom.

Jesus promised spiritual insight to those who obeyed His Word, "He that hath My commandments, and keepeth them, he it is that loveth Me: and he that loveth Me shall be loved of My Father, and I will love him, and will manifest Myself to him" (John 14:21). The only disciple described as "whom Jesus loved," John received an amazing grasp of spiritual truth, including the message of Revelation. Had not Daniel been called a man "greatly beloved" just before receiving the revelation of the Seventy Weeks (Daniel 9:23)? Oswald Chambers once said, "God does not have favorites, but He does have intimates."

John, who was given the Patmos vision of the awesome Christ, (Revelation 1:9-18), and who saw the Lamb upon the throne surrounded by myriads of adoring angels (Revelation 5:1-14), was certainly qualified to soar eagle-high to unveil Christ's unclouded magnificence. How fitting that He who leaned on the Master's bosom in the Upper Room was chosen to write about the only-begotten God who was "in the bosom of the Father" (1:18).

Significant omissions and additions

No genealogy appears in John, for God has neither father nor grandfather. Thus, no birth account nor lineage. Without beginning, from eternity He is God. John's opening statement, "In the beginning was the Word," echoes the first four words of Genesis, "In the beginning God." John says this Word was God, Maker of all, Who became flesh and dwelt among us (1:1-14).

There's no temptation, for God cannot be tempted. No parables. In His prayer life Jesus seems to speak to His Father as an equal rather than as a suppliant.

John does not include the transfiguration. To him, the wonder was not that Jesus' glory suddenly shone through that midnight hour, dazzling the three disciples to the ground, but rather that the brilliance of His deity could be concealed for 33 years within His flesh. Though he may have referred to the transfiguration when he wrote, "We beheld His glory," he certainly had in mind the splendor of His moral character, full of grace and truth (1:14).

Much Galilean ministry is omitted. Unlike Matthew, Mark, and Luke which deal more with Jesus' activity in Galilee, John, apart from 2:1-12, 4:3-54, 6:1-71, and 7:1-9, centers His ministry in Jerusalem and Judea. He makes references to three Passovers (2:13, 6:4, 12:1) and to the Feasts of Tabernacles (7:2) and of Dedication (10:22), whereas in Matthew, Mark, and Luke we read of only one Passover visit preceding the Passion. John shows thorough familiarity with Messianic ideas, Jewish customs, and Jerusalem topography, such as the pools of Bethesda (5:2) and of Siloam (9:7), Solomon's porch (10:23), the brook Kidron (18:1), and the Pavement (19:13). Indeed, "He came unto His own" (1:11). When His own rejected Him, the offer was then extended to all who would welcome Him (1:12). Though Matthew was written for Jews, Mark for Romans, and Luke for Greeks, John was written for the world. Whosoever, Jew or Gentile, could come. The word, "world," occurs 78 times, more than any other major word except "believe." Only in John do we learn that the superscription was in three languages: Hebrew, Latin, and Greek.

Many miracles and sayings found in Matthew, Mark, and Luke are not included in John who seems to assume his readers' familiarity with much of the material of Jesus' life. When John says that John the Baptist was not yet in prison (3:24), he doesn't tell the story of John's imprisonment because he's sure others have read it already. When John relates that Jesus was led to Annas first (18:13), he assumes his readers know that Jesus was tried before Caiaphas, but did not know about His prior appearance before Annas, so details a fact that Matthew, Mark, and Luke did not record. John wrote his Gospel at least 20 years after Matthew, Mark, and Luke, organizing his content to include much that was new and to avoid repetition of earlier data. Some suggest this accounts for the absence in John of any mention of demons. However, supplementing Matthew, Mark, and Luke was secondary to his main purpose, which was to choose information demonstrating the deity of Jesus.

An interesting variation occurs in the story of Mary of Bethany anointing Jesus. As related by Matthew, Mary poured the precious ointment "on His head" (26:7). Is not the head where a king is anointed, and does not Matthew feature Jesus as King? But John informs us, complementing Matthew's account, that Mary anointed the *feet* of Jesus (12:3). Worship bows at the feet of Deity, which is where John locates the anointing.

Only in John do we find Jesus washing the disciples' feet, an act symbolizing the condescension of God the Son. Only in John do we read the discourses in the Upper Room, on the way to Gethsemane, and the intercessory prayer prior to entering the garden. These lessons cover five complete chapters (13-17), a sizable section of the Gospel, all uttered within the span of just a few hours, and all omitted from Matthew, Mark, and Luke.

John differs strikingly from the other Gospels in the Passion account. Significant omissions are compatible with Deity. No cry of Jesus, "If it be possible, let this cup pass from Me." No sweat of blood. No crying of women. No angel appearing to strengthen Him. No compelling of Simon of Cyrene to bear His cross. No cry of God-forsakenness. No mocking of the Son of God by the crowd. No non-breaking of His legs (19:32, 33).

Rather, Deity asserts itself. John includes facts not found elsewhere. The soldiers trying to arrest Him in the Garden, fall backward to the ground at His statement, "I am He." His robe is seamless, a garment befitting a noble personage (19:23). Though He cries, "I thirst," He does so to fulfill Scripture. His cry of victory, "It is finished," followed by His cry of dismissal of His spirit, demonstrates His earlier affirmation, "I lay down my life, that I might take it again. No man taketh it from me, but I lay it down of myself. I have power to lay it down, and I have power to take it again" (John 10:17, 18).

The epilogue (21) seems an anticlimactic appendage after the convincing confession of doubting Thomas and the ringing statement of John's purpose in writing, at the end of chapter 20. How fitting to end there! But then come two episodes unique to John: the miraculous catch of 153 fish, and the restoration of Peter. This final chapter is necessary on two counts. First, the disciples, about to embark on the Great Commission, needed a reminder that to catch men in the gospel net would require the power of Christ's deity. Second, had the Gospel ended at chapter 20, readers' last memory of Peter would have been a blaspheming, bitterly weeping, Christ-denying coward. Without Peter's restoration we would puzzle at his leadership in the upper room, his preaching at Pentecost, and his prominence in early Acts.

SIMPLICITY

John uses simple words to express profound thought—so plain that a child can read them, yet so profound that no scholar can fully fathom them. Note the simplicity, yet sublimity, of some of John's key words, many of them monosyllabics in English, and found more often in John than in all other three Gospels combined: believe (98 times), world (78), know (55), life (50), witness (46), glory (42), love (40), sent (38), light (23), work (23), abide (20), and sign (17). The conflict of opposites is characteristic: light vs. darkness, love vs. hate, life vs. death, flesh vs. spirit, slavery vs. liberty.

An example of his depth of meaning is his use of "word," which occurs 40 times in John's Gospel. Professor Dr. Gordon H. Clark says that "the Greek term 'logos' can be translated by forty different English words. Liddel and Scott's great lexicon has more than five columns, each 90 lines long, of its various meanings." [1] Here is a sampling of its meanings: computation, account, measure, sum, consideration, value, reputation, argument, principle, law, thesis, hypothesis, narrative, oration, phrase, message, dialogue, proverb, relation, formula, proportion, reflection, debate, language, wisdom.

In philosophy Philo is known for his use of the term "Logos." In his view a system of intermediaries exists between God and the world, of which the "Logos" is at once the chief and the totality. The Logos has been called "a second God, the highest of the angels, the original pattern of the world, and the force which fashions it." [2] It is not clear if the Logos is personal or impersonal, but John, who seems to have a philosophical bent, pours new significance into the term. As used in the first chapter of his Gospel, the Word, Who became flesh, is a means of revelation and communication. Jesus is the personal manifestation of the Father. He is the Father's message. He is the exegesis of the eternal God (1:1, 14, 18).

---

1. *The Trinity Review*, November/December 1984, No. 40, p. 1.

2. Martin, Clark, Clarke, and Ruddick, *A History of Philosophy*, F.S. Crofts Co., 1941, p. 241.

No parables occur in John. He prefers discourses as the vehicle of explaining the mysteries of light, life, and other abstract concepts. These extended dissertations replace parables and maxims. "Parable" in 10:6 (KJV) should read "proverb."

SEVENS

A.W. Pink, in *Why Four Gospels?*, says that John is fond of the number seven, which typifies perfection. Seven times we read, "These things have I spoken unto you." Seven times Jesus addressed the woman at the well. Seven times Jesus spoke of Himself as the Bread of Life. Seven times He made mention of the "hour" which was to see the accomplishment of His work. Here are the most significant of the sevens: seven miracles, seven witnesses, and seven "I am's."

Seven miracles

Instead of grouping miracles as Matthew does, John uses them selectively, amplifying several with theological discourse in order to convince his readers that Jesus is the Son of God (20:30, 31). Out of dozens of signs John chooses seven, all performed before the crucifixion, five exclusive to his Gospel.

- Turning water into wine at Cana (2:1-11)
- Healing a nobleman's son (4:46-54)
- Healing a cripple at the pool of Bethesda (5:1-47)
- Feeding the 5,000 (6:1-14)
- Walking on water (6:15-22)
- Healing a man born blind (9:1-42)
- Raising Lazarus from the dead at Bethany (11:1-46).

From wedding (Cana) to grave (Bethany) Jesus is Master.

Seven witnesses

The word "witness" occurs more in John than in all other Gospels combined, 46 times in noun or verb form. Though the Scriptures (5:39), His heavenly Father (5:37), His works (10:25), and the Holy Spirit (15:26) all bear witness to the truth of Jesus' claims, the following seven persons also testify:

- John the Baptist calls Jesus "The Lamb of God." John is the only Gospel in which He receives this title (1:29; 5:33).
- Nathaniel calls Jesus "Son of God" and "King of Israel" (1:49).

- The Samaritan woman witnessed, "Come, see a man, which told me all things that ever I did: is not this the Christ?" (4:29).
- Peter affirmed, "We believe and are sure that Thou art that Christ, the Son of the living God" (6:69).
- Martha, just prior to the raising of her brother, Lazarus, said, "I believe that Thou art the Christ, the Son of God, which should come into the world" (11:27).
- Thomas, at seeing the scars in Jesus' hands and side, said, "My Lord and my God" (20:28).
- And the author of the Gospel, John himself, at the end of His story, wrote, "This is the disciple which testifieth of these things, and wrote these things: and we know that His testimony is true" (21:24).

A boy, not yet in his teens, a key witness in an important lawsuit, was subjected to rigorous cross-examination by a lawyer who tried hard, but was unable to shake the lad's clear, damaging testimony. Sternly the lawyer made an accusation. "Your father has been telling you how to testify, hasn't he?" When the lad admitted it, the lawyer smugly smiled, "Now just tell us what your father told you to say?"

The boy replied, "Father told me that the lawyers might try to tangle me, but if I would just be careful and tell the truth, I could say the same thing every time." John maintained the truth of his testimony till his dying breath seventy years later.

Seven "I AM's"

"I AM" was the name by which God revealed Himself to Moses in the burning bush (Exodus 3:14). Jesus' self-appropriation seven times of this title was nothing short of claims to deity.

- I AM *the Bread of Life* (6:35).

Though the miracle of the feeding of the 5,000 occurs in all four Gospels, only John follows the story with a long discourse on Jesus as the Living Bread.

- I AM *the Light of the World* (8:12).

The word "light" is found more in John than in all other three Gospels together. The opening chapter declares Jesus the Light, enlightening every person entering the world (1:4-9). Men hide from Him because they love darkness more than light.

- I AM *the Door* (10:9).
- I AM *the Good Shepherd* (10:11).
- I AM *the Resurrection and the Life* (11:25).

"Life" is another word found more in John than in all other Gospels combined. Life is a mystery. At the very outset John states that Jesus is the creator of all life (1:3, 4). He is the source of both physical and spiritual life. This claim was made in connection with the raising of Lazarus from the dead.

- I AM *the Way, the Truth, and the Life* (14:6).

The word "truth" occurs rarely in any of the other Gospels, but more than 20 times in John. Though the expression "verily" (meaning "amen" or "of a truth") occurs many times in the other Gospels, it always appears in singular form. Only in John, do we have its double form, "verily, verily." This double affirmation (about 25 times) emphasizes Jesus' title as the Truth.

Since Jesus is the Truth, He knows all. "Know" occurs over 50 times in this Gospel. He knew the character of Nathaniel before meeting him (1:47). He knew what was in man (2:25). He knew the marital status of the Samaritan woman (4:17). He knew the man at the pool of Bethesda had been an invalid a long time (5:6). He knew who would betray Him (13:11). He knew that Peter, despite his blatant denials, loved Him (21:17).

- I AM *the True Vine* (15:5).

FATHER-RELATED

Jesus speaks of God as "my Father" over 30 times. He repeatedly highlights His oneness with the Father.

This relationship extended from eternity past

From the beginning Jesus fellowshiped with the Father (1:1). Jesus prayed for the Father to glorify Him with the glory "which I had with Thee before the world began" (17:1). Jesus also mentioned the Father's love which He enjoyed "before the foundation of the world" (17:24). Jesus often spoke of coming down from heaven (3:13, 17, 19; 6:38, 51). As the only begotten Son in the bosom of the Father, He manifested His Father (1:18).

This relationship involved a mission from the Father

More than 30 times Jesus claimed to be sent of the Father. For example, "Neither came I of Myself, but He sent me" (8:42). "I am from Him, and He hath sent Me" (7:29). "I go unto Him that sent Me" (7:33). His mission involved a message to be proclaimed, and a sacrifice to be offered.

As to His message, Jesus said, "For He Whom God hath sent speaketh the words of God" (3:34). He constantly appealed for faith in His message and in the Father Who sent Him. "He that heareth my Word, and believeth on Him that sent me, hath everlasting life" (5:24). But to reject Jesus' words was to reject the Father's teaching.

As to His sacrifice, He was commissioned to give His life a ransom for sin. "God sent not His son into the world to condemn the world; but that the world through Him might be saved" (3:17). Aware of His goal, He frequently used the words, "the hour" or "my hour." He let nothing swerve Him from His conscious progress toward the cross which He regarded as the central hour of His entire ministry (2:4; 7:6, 30; 8:20; 12:23; 13:1; 17:1).

This relationship involved absolute submission to the Father

Jesus never acted independently. He never uttered a word, nor performed an act unless under the conscious direction of His heavenly Father. Full responsibility for all His words and works pointed upward to the One Who sent Him.

Theologians speak of the subordination of the Son to the Father. They do not mean that Jesus was less than God, or inferior to the Father. They mean that for 33 years He subordinated Himself to the authority of the Father, doing only as the Father commanded. While remaining fully God, He gave up the independent use of His attributes, assigning that prerogative to his Father, and submitting to Him in every area. He said:

- "I came down from heaven, not to do Mine own will, but the will of Him that sent Me" (6:38).
- "My doctrine is not Mine, but His that sent Me" (7:16).
- "I must work the works of Him that sent Me" (9:4).
- "Even as the Father said unto Me, so I speak" (12:50).
- "The words that I speak unto you I speak not of Myself: but the Father that dwelleth in Me, He doeth the works" (14:10).

Such statements give force to John's version of the Great Commission, "As My Father hath sent Me, even so send I you" (20:21). Are we willing to say and do only what He bids us? Are we prepared to be messenger boys and girls for Jesus? Can we say, "I do always those things that please Him" (8:29)?

This relationship involved equality of the Son with the Father

The Son had power to do what only God can do. He claimed that some day He would raise the dead by His choice (5:28, 29), and also that some day He would be the Judge of mankind (5:22, 26, 27). He claimed to be the only way to the Father (14:6), also that whoever had seen Him had seen the Father also (14:9). He claimed that He and His Father would indwell believers (14:23).

The Son claimed oneness with the Father in sending the Holy Spirit (14:16). Luke's references to the Holy Spirit deal mainly with the enabling of the Holy Spirit on the ministry of Jesus, especially at the beginning, while John's teachings dwell on the person, deity and ministry of the third Person of the Trinity. Jesus claimed to be co-dispatcher with the Father in sending the Holy Spirit into the world on the Day of Pentecost (16:7).

Jesus claimed equality with the Father, and thus to be God. The leaders so understood Jesus, and for that reason, on at least two occasions tried to kill Him. The first time, "They sought the more to kill Him, because He not only had broken the sabbath, but said also that God was His Father, making Himself equal with God" (5:18). The second incident began with Jesus claiming, "I and My Father are one." The leaders then took up stones to kill Him, "because Thou, being a man, maketh Thyself God" (10:33).

Because of Jesus' equality with the Father "all men should honor the Son, even as they honor the Father" (5:23). And the verse goes on to the logical impossibility of acknowledging the Father while rejecting the Son. "He that honoreth not the Son honoreth not the Father which hath sent Him."

Though believers in Jesus are called sons of God, their sonship differs from Jesus' sonship as day from night. Jesus Christ is the unique, incarnate Son of God and thus different from believers in their relationship as sons of God. We are adopted into God's family in time whereas Jesus is God's eternal Son, whose life and deity never began but have always been.

Many cults try to make man some sort of a god. Says Walter

Martin, "Herbert W. Armstrong's Worldwide Church of God, for instance, teaches that there is a 'god family' in which all Armstrongists will eventually share. They will become as much deity as the Father and Son. . . . Christian Science, the Unity School of Christianity, the Science of Mind or Religious Science, New Thought Metaphysics, and so on, believe that all humans have within themselves the 'Christ consciousness' or 'Christ idea,' which is allegedly the true divinity of men. They maintain that Jesus Christ possessed this divinity to a greater degree than others, which is what sets Him apart, but none of these groups confess the eternal deity of Jesus Christ, the Word of God made flesh, and His unique relationship to the Father as the 'only begotten Son.'" [3] Martin warns against those who teach the "little gods" theory which asserts that the Christian is as much an incarnation of God as is Jesus of Nazareth. No Biblical text suggests that redeemed men are or ever will be gods. Such teaching he calls idolatrous and blasphemous. [4]

BELIEF

John desires his readers to come to abiding faith in Jesus. Faith is in the central concept in the Gospel of John. The word "believe" occurs 98 times, more frequently than any other word, and more frequently than in any other Bible book. Dr. Merrill Tenney titled his commentary on John, *The Gospel of Belief.*

Mixed reception

Jesus' claims brought controversy as He offered Himself as their Messiah. The reactions of His hearers differed. Tenney lists 26 conversations in the fourth Gospel which Jesus had with all types of people, like Nicodemus and the Samaritan woman. Some interviews were private, others public. Some were casual, other calculated. One was at noon, another at night. Some resulted in immediate acceptance; others, in rejection. Three times we read of a division among the people because of Him (7:43; 9:16; 10:19). After the raising of Lazarus, many believed on Him; others plotted His death (11:45, 53).

---

3. *The Agony of Deceit*, edited by Michael Horton, Moody Press, 1990, p. 92.
4. Ibid., pp. 100, 101.

His own received Him not.

No other Gospel mentions as frequently the plotting of Jewish leadership against Jesus, and their responsibility for His crucifixion. In the prologue John pictures Jesus as rejected. "He came unto His own, and His own received Him not" (1:11). The two "own"s in this verse differ in gender. The first "own" is neuter, but the second is masculine. Jesus came to His own things or household (people and things), but His own people would not receive Him. Phillips translates it, "He came into His own creation, and His own people would not accept Him."

But creation recognized Him. A star led to His birthplace. Waves upheld Him as He walked on the sea. A wind calmed at His beckon. A fig tree withered at His word. Fish obeyed Him, filling the disciples' nets after a night of fruitless toil. A dove landed on Him at His baptism. A cock crowed twice during Peter's denial. The sun hid its face in darkness during the last hour of the crucifixion. At both His death and resurrection the earth quaked. This acceptance by creation, while people rejected, echoed Isaiah's indictment, "The ox knoweth his owner, and the ass his master's crib: but Israel doth not know, my people doth not consider" (1:3). Though Jesus' own people turned Him down, John wanted the world to know that "as many as received Him" (Jew or Gentile) became the true children of God (1:12). John's Gospel contains the word "world" nearly 80 times.

A retired jockey showed up at a mission service on Palm Sunday. After the story of Jesus' entry into Jerusalem, he commented, "What a jockey Jesus would have made! I know what He was riding. It was a Syrian colt. Once I had a drove of those beasts to break in. Imagine Jesus sitting on one that nobody had ever ridden before, and all those youngsters running in front and waving palms. Yet Jesus was holding the colt meek as anything." The jockey paused a moment, then added, "I say—if He could do that with that bit of horseflesh, I reckon He could do something with me." And the jockey committed himself to Christ.

John's Gospel headlines the news—no one less than God, the Son, has paid a visit to this planet. The Word became flesh. God became man. For 33 years, the world's Creator walked and worked on the very earth He had created. Sadly, His creatures rejected Him and engineered His death. But His death was not final. He turned tragedy into triumph. Through His death He paid the penalty for our sins, then rose triumphantly from the grave. John wrote his Gospel to create faith in Jesus, Who has a right to our full and abiding allegiance. If Jesus is God, then no idol should consume our interest. John wants all people everywhere to confess with Thomas, "My Lord and my God."

Any word used nearly 100 times in a book of the Bible, as "believe" is in this Gospel, deserves more than passing attention. Just what does it mean to believe in Jesus?

10

What It Means to Believe

T he first commercial jet airline service in the U.S. began in 1958 with the flight of the Boeing 707. A month later a passenger on a propeller-driven DC-6 airliner, discovering the man sitting beside him was a Boeing engineer, asked him about the new jet aircraft. The engineer spoke convincingly about the thorough testing Boeing had done on jet engines. The other man asked, "Have you ever flown on the new 707 jet?" The engineer paused, "I think I'll wait until it's been in service awhile." Though the engineer worked for Boeing and knew firsthand his company's long experience with the manufacture of aircraft engines, he still lacked full faith in the 707 jet.

For many folks it takes a lot of faith just to enter a plane. Over 100 million in the USA have never flown, mainly because of fear. They like *terra firma*, the more *firma*, the less *terra*. A few years ago a *Fly Without Fear* club was organized in New York city to help people overcome their fear of flying. Fifty people paid a $40 registration fee, and $10 for each counseling session during the four months of group therapy. Success rate was around 90%. A stewardess on their first flight commented, "I've never seen a happier group of passengers."

Flying in a plane and becoming a Christian have a lot in common. Just as we need faith to board a plane, so we need faith in Jesus to land us in heaven. But what is faith? Faith is a word freely used, but often carelessly and imprecisely. In tough times we are told, "Just have faith." Faith has become a nebulous commodity that will transport us safely through life's difficulties and death's beckon. Faith needs some rethinking.

FAITH REQUIRES AN OBJECT

"Faith is bunk," exclaimed a very practical man, adding, "I believe only in things I can see." But a friend reminded the skeptic, "In the last week you've pressed the light switch countless times without looking to see if the wires were up between the office and the pole outside. You've asked the gas station attendant to put in 10 gallons without checking the pump. You've taken out a certificate of deposit without scanning the bank's balance sheet. You've ridden the elevator several times a day without examining its cable to make sure it wasn't frayed. You've eaten every noon in a restaurant without a guarantee that someone in the kitchen had not sprinkled arsenic on the food. You've made a flight to Chicago and back without inspecting the DC-10's three jet engines." The skeptic really had exercised faith, and his faith in each case had an object, whether the power company, the gas station's pumping system, the bank, the elevator, the restaurant, or the airline.

Transitive verbs are followed by an object. To say, "The carpenter built," is incomplete. What did he build—a chair, a door, a house? The verb "believe" requires an object. Faith is not some ethereal nebula, free floating, existing apart from an object. Faith, even misplaced faith, must rest on something.

FAITH REQUIRES AN OBJECT WHICH IS ULTIMATELY A PERSON

Faith isn't really in the power company, but in the people who operate it. Faith basically rests not in the pump, but in the owner of the service station, in those who manage the bank's finances, who service the elevator, who handle the restaurant's food. Ultimate responsibility traces back to people.

An airline thought it had perfected an automatic system, making the presence of a pilot unnecessary. As the passengers waited for takeoff, the loudspeaker announced, "Everything on this plane is automatic. No pilot is needed to take off, fly, or land. So you have nothing to worry about—nothing to worry about—nothing to worry about." Airline safety rests on people—those who manufacture, inspect, service, overhaul, fuel the plane, and pre-eminently on the pilot who maneuvers the aircraft through the skies, and also on the air controllers who keep planes from colliding. Hundreds of persons share responsibility. Faith resides ultimately in people.

Saving faith has Jesus Christ, God's Son, for its object

Faith in one's own self is misplaced for we cannot save ourselves. Faith in faith itself may sound romantic and mystical, but is wholly subjective and futile. True Christian faith is objective, resting in an historical, concrete object outside of oneself—the person of Jesus Christ. Though the entire revelation of God as found in the Bible is the object of faith, that revelation centers in a person. The main character of the Scriptures is God's eternal Son. In the upper room that first Easter night the risen Jesus showed how the three major divisions of the Old Testament spoke of Him, especially His death and resurrection, "All things must be fulfilled, which were written in the law of Moses, and in the prophets, and in the psalms, concerning Me. Then opened He their understanding, that they might understand the Scriptures" (Luke 24:44, 45).

Some interpret faith in Jesus to mean that He is merely the example of someone who had faith and whose faith we are to copy. But faith in Jesus goes beyond imitation of a model. He is the object of our faith. On Him we depend as our Savior. Christian dogma leads to the person of Jesus. Philip, meeting the Ethiopian eunuch in the Gaza desert, from the book of Isaiah preached to Him Jesus (Acts 8:35). The philosophers at Athens described Paul as "a setter forth of strange gods: because he preached unto them Jesus . . ." (17:18). The best-known verse in the Bible focuses on Jesus, "For God so loved the world, that He gave His only begotten Son, that whosoever believeth in Him, should not perish, but have everlasting life" (John 3:16).

Most of the Apostles' Creed centers on Jesus. Except for a brief opening clause affirming faith in God the Father Almighty, and the final sentence averring faith in the Holy Spirit, the main, middle and longest section refers to "Jesus Christ, His only Son, our Lord, Who was conceived by the Holy Spirit, born of the Virgin Mary, suffered under Pontius Pilate, was crucified, dead, and buried; He descended into hell; and the third day He rose again from the dead; He ascended into heaven, and sitteth on the right hand of God, the Father Almighty; from thence He shall come to judge the quick and the dead."

FAITH MUST BE BASED ON KNOWLEDGE OF ITS OBJECT

True faith is not blind. Faith in a person without evidence of his competence is presumption. Would you permit a little boy, who wanted to be a doctor but who had never held a scalpel in his hand, to operate on you? Even if urged to "just have faith"? To do so would be sheer folly, not faith.

A nervous lady, walking toward a commercial airliner, saw the pilot heading that way too. "Be careful, captain," she said, "this is my first flight." The pilot replied, "Don't feel too badly. This is my first flight too." Airline regulations assure the qualifications of airline pilots. But suppose as you were about to board a small, privately owned plane, you were told that your pilot would be a ten-year-old girl whose ambition was to become a pilot, but who had never sat at the controls of a plane. Would you climb on board, even if bystanders begged, "just have faith"? To climb aboard would be utter insanity.

Creed or Christ?

Ever hear expressions like "No creed but Christ"? Or, "Faith is not a belief in a proposition, but trust in a person." Though they sound pious, these statements are half-truths. Trust in a person is a meaningless phrase unless that trust involves knowledge about that person. For example, to have intelligent faith in Jesus, we need the information found in the Apostles' Creed. At a denomination's annual conference a liberal theologian opposed precision in defining doctrines about Jesus. Rejecting such terminology as the deity of Christ, substitutionary atonement, and bodily resurrection, he suggested instead the simple statement that "Christ is all we need." Whereupon a pastor from the denomination's evangelical wing took to the floor to ask the pointed question, "Which Christ?" It is not a choice between creed or Christ. It is both and: both creed and Christ: both belief in a proposition and trust in a person. The statements in a creed identify the qualifications of the person in whom we place our trust. Saving faith involves assent to certain propositions about Christ.

Mark Twain once defined faith as "believing in something you know really isn't true." But valid faith is just the opposite, not blind, but based on fact. That's why we should have some prior knowledge of Jesus if our faith in Him is to be intelligent. We don't have to be a whiz in theology, but we must have enough information to confidently place our trust in Him for our salvation. For example, we must know about the incarnation, realizing that Jesus came in the flesh (1 Jn. 4:2), stooping to the level of creaturehood, making Himself man.

Also, we must know that Jesus was, and is, God forever. We must recognize the deity of Him Who became so tired that He fell asleep in a tossing boat, Who became thirsty, and Who wept at Lazarus' grave. Though man, He ever remained God. If just on the same level as Plato or Lincoln, how is He worthy of our faith?

We must know about the atonement of Jesus, namely that He shed His blood on the cross as our substitute to pay the penalty for our sins. No mere martyr unable to avoid His fate, nor example to show how he should face death, He was rather a sacrifice, satisfying divine justice and reconciling us to God.

In addition, we must know about the resurrection of Jesus, who, rising bodily, left behind an empty tomb, and appeared repeatedly and indisputably to His followers. The New Testament says, "That if thou shalt confess with thy mouth the Lord Jesus and shalt believe in thine heart that God hath raised Him from the dead, thou shalt be saved" (Rom. 10:9).

Christianity is not anti-intellectual. John wrote his Gospel to provide evidence for our faith. At the end he gave a clear statement as to why he wrote: "Many other signs truly did Jesus in the presence of His disciples, which are not written in this book: But these are written, that ye might believe that Jesus is the Christ, the Son of God; and that believing ye might have life through His name" (John 20:30, 31). Three words in this statement of purpose—signs, believe, life—form a logical sequence. John wished to lead his readers into a settled conviction on the basis of actual, historic events which signified that the Person performing them was none less than God incarnate. And believing was the means to a greater end—eternal life—which John defined as knowing "Thee, the only true God, and Him Whom Thou didst send, even Jesus Christ" (17:3).

Says Dr. Merrill Tenney, "Belief presupposes that which will produce it. The Scriptures never demand belief without furnishing adequate reason for committal to the person or proposition toward which the belief should be directed." [1] Faith must be based on knowledge of its object.

FAITH IS ONLY AS VALID AS ITS OBJECT

A bridge on the Connecticut Turnpike collapsed a few years ago, hurtling several vehicles into the river and killing some occupants. Nothing was wrong with the faith of those drivers, who drove onto the bridge. The trouble rested with the bridge, a section of which gave way. Faith is only as sound as its object. Paul Little hypothesized: "We might think of a diseased little girl whose primitive father takes her through the jungle to the witch doctor. The father may have implicit faith in the concoction being brewed to cure her. But no matter how much he believes in the potion, his faith won't save his daughter's life if the brew is poison. Faith is no more valid than the object in which it is placed. His faith is no more than superstition." [2]

On your way to mail a letter you meet someone who suggests that you drop the letter into a nearby garbage can. "Just have faith," he says. All the faith in the world in that garbage can will never ensure the safe arrival of that letter. An official post office box is the proper object of faith for the mailing of a letter. Misplaced faith renders faith null and void.

An elderly lady in all good faith handed over her life savings to a crooked financial adviser. Her trust, complete as it was, did not prevent him from embezzling all her money. Her faith would prove effective only if placed in an honest adviser.

Intensity of belief does not create faith

In our day of widespread relativism many naively think that to believe a thing true or untrue makes it so. Someone remarks, "I don't believe in hell," and concludes that he has wiped it out of existence and need not worry about it anymore. But according to God's Word the fact of hell remains despite the depth of our unbe-

---

1. *John: The Gospel of Belief*, Eerdmans, 1948, p. 33.
2. *How to Give Away Your Faith*, Inter-Varsity Press, 1966, p. 106.

lief. No matter how intense our faith or skepticism may be, we cannot create or destroy objective realities.

A young man visiting a church, though a total stranger, was able to wrangle free room and board for two months before disappearing with his host's cash and jewelry. The elderly widow who had given him shelter explained, "He was such a nice boy. I had total faith in him. He even wore a pin, 'Jesus saves.'"

A weak faith in a strong object is superior to a strong faith in a weak object

Two sailors, shipwrecked and floundering on a lonely sea, spotted two rafts floating nearby. One, selecting the sturdier-looking, thought, "That'll hold me up." Soon he was sitting on it. But moments later, the raft sank. His strong faith rested on an unreliable object. The other sailor shakily grabbed the remaining fragile-appearing raft, doubting it could sustain his weight. To his amazement the raft kept him afloat till he was rescued later. His trust, though weak, was in a dependable object.

Jesus is the raft that saves. Even weak faith in Jesus, the strong raft, will get us to heaven, whereas the firmest faith in Buddha, Confucius, some guru, or other fallible earthly religious leader will not avail to land us in heaven.

FAITH REQUIRES AN ACT OF COMMITTAL TO ITS OBJECT

If someone announced in a meeting that a warning had just been received that a bomb would explode in that room in five minutes, it would be easy to tell who believed the threat, not just giving it mental assent, by noting who dashed for the exits.

Mere intellectual understanding of the gospel falls short of saving faith. The demons believe there is one God, and tremble (James 2:19). They understand the gospel better than some theologians, but still are not saved. Saving faith demands more than mental acquiescence to the plan of salvation.

Knowing that a letter, properly addressed and dropped into a mailbox, will reach a friend does not get that letter to its destination. Such knowledge must be followed by committing the letter to a mailbox and postal system. Understanding that a doctor's prescription can cure an illness will not help if the medicine is purchased and left on the shelf. The sick man must commit himself to the doctor's prescription by taking it.

Possession of a plane ticket does not guarantee a passenger's arrival at the flight's destination. The passenger must commit himself to plane and pilot by boarding the aircraft. Dr. Vernon Grounds, President Emeritus of Denver Baptist Seminary, illustrates the need for committal. "Suppose I am busy in New York city till evening, and wishing to reach Chicago by midnight, I learn from my travel agent that the last available plane leaves LaGuardia at 10 p.m. So I make a reservation and buy my ticket. On that day, I arrive at LaGuardia in plenty of time, check in and get my boarding pass. To make sure I'm at the right gate I ask a couple of passengers if this is the 10 p.m. plane to Chicago. They tell me it is. Mentally I review the situation. The travel agent, the airline clerk, the passengers all assure me this is the 10 p.m. flight for Chicago. I look at my ticket. It reads '10 p.m., Chicago.' My boarding pass lists my seat number on the plane. Without a doubt this is the 10 p.m. flight to Chicago and I have a guaranteed, assigned seat. Suddenly the airline clerk announces that the flight is ready to board. Passengers begin moving through the doorway that leads to the plane. I stand there, shaking my head in sincere and genuine agreement—this is the 10 p.m. flight to Chicago. I watch all the passengers move through the gate, which is then shut. I'm able to see the plane accelerate down the runway and zoom off into the night toward Chicago without me, as I keep on assuring myself in sincere and genuine agreement that this is the plane to Chicago." Grounds comments, "The illustration is a little absurd. But it brings out a vital point. Mere intellectual assent is not enough. If I want to reach Chicago, I must do more than agree in genuine sincerity with the correct information. I must personally get on board the right plane."

Then Grounds adds, "Thus it is with salvation—with becoming a Christian. I must do more than assent to correct information about Jesus Christ. I must do more than agree with a proper doctrinal statement. I must do more than believe that Jesus is God Incarnate, that He died on the cross as a sacrifice for my sin, that He rose the third day from the grave to grant forgiveness to all who seek mercy. I must do more than subscribe to an orthodox creed. I must personally accept Jesus Christ as my Savior. I must board His plane called 'salvation' with Him as my 'Pilot' who can land me safely in heaven. What a tragedy it is that there are people in our churches who mistake intellectual agreement for personal acceptance. They accept the message of the Bible, the word of the pastor, the testimony of fellow-passengers, but they are tragically not headed for heaven. They have never climbed on board."

Lawrence E. Nelson said that though Lord Byron was moved by the Bible, using its stories as the basis for some of his poetry, his libertine lifestyle was evidence that he did not follow the precepts of the Bible. "Of the Satan school Byron might be, but he knew his Bible. 'I am a great reader of those books,' he noted, 'and had read them through and through before I was eight years old.' . . . Many of the Psalms he knew by memory, and when a Methodistically inclined physician sought to convert him, Byron discussed matters with him for hours at a time, frequently correcting the zealot's biblical quotations." [3]

Paul Little reported that "Benjamin Franklin wrote commentaries on the Bible, but as far as we know he never became a Christian." [4]

Though the verb "believe" is found 98 times in John's Gospel, its corresponding noun form "faith" is completely absent. Concordances show that "faith" occurs in Matthew, Mark, and Luke, but completely skips John, then resumes in Acts, Romans, and in later books. John's choices of the verb (which in grammar denotes action), with his complete avoidance of the noun form, suggests that faith requires a step of entrusting. Also, John follows the verb "believe" with the preposition "into" 36 times, reinforcing the idea of committal. In John "believe into" is usually followed by "Jesus" or an equivalent pronoun or phrase.

In his book, *Life in Christ,* in which he examines the New Testament phrases that describe our position in Christ, Dr. John Stott tells how one missionary translated "believe into." John Paton, born in Scotland in 1824, served ten years as a Glasgow city missionary, later studied theology and medicine, then after graduation and ordination set sail for the New Hebrides as a Presbyterian missionary. Despite the death of his young wife and five-week-old son and the threats against his life, he persisted in his labors. While working in his home on the translation of John's Gospel, he was puzzling over the evangelist's frequent expression, "believe into," which first occurs in 1:12. How to translate it? The islanders were cannibals, did not trust each other, and had no

---

3. *Our Roving Bible*, Abingdon-Cokesbury, 1945, pp. 152-4.
4. *How to Give Away Your Faith*, pp. 124, 5.

word for "trust" in their language. Just then his servant came in. "What am I doing?" he asked the national. The servant replied that he was sitting at his desk. Paton then raised both feet off the floor, sat on his chair, and asked, "What am I doing now?" In reply the servant used an expression which meant "to lean your whole weight upon." Patton used this expression throughout John's Gospel to translate "believe into." [5] Saving faith is resting faith, a complete reliance upon the Savior.

Some folks believe in Jesus the same way they believe in Plato, Caesar, Napoleon, Washington, Lincoln, or Churchill, merely as a character in history. But they are not trusting in that historical personage to do anything for them now. Faith may be defined as the awareness of the mind in comprehending Jesus Christ as our only Savior from sin, and the action of the will in appropriating His finished work in loving response. Two elements stand out in that definition: information and action. It's not enough to know the data that Jesus died for our sins and rose from the dead for our forgiveness. On the basis of those simple facts we must reach out with the will and accept Him as our crucified and risen Lord. This reaching out in saving faith is expressed in various ways, like receiving Jesus (Jn. 1:12); following Jesus (1:43); looking to Jesus (3:14); drinking Jesus, the Water of Life (4:14); coming to Christ (5:40); eating Jesus, the Bread of Life (6:51); and knowing Jesus (17:3).

On a visit to Niagara Falls I saw up on wires over a downtown street a replica of Blondin, the famous tightrope walker. Nicknamed because of his flowing, pale-yellow locks, and in his mid-thirties, Blondin came to America in 1849 under contract to Barnum of circus fame. After viewing the Falls, he volunteered to cross the gorge on a cable. Bookies offered heavy odds against his ever attempting it, and still bigger odds against his survival, if ever he did try. With borrowed money he purchased cable 1500 feet long and three inches thick, which he lashed to an iron shaft cemented deep in rock on the Canadian side. A horse-powered winch pulled the cable tight on the American side. The cable sagged some 50 feet over the middle of the gorge and swayed like a branch in the breeze.

His first performance began at 4 p.m. on June 30 with a brass band bursting into the national anthem. Blondin pranced out from

5. Tyndale, 1991, p. 25.

the American side, clad in pink tights and gripping a long balancing pole. Amidst exclamations from the crowd, he marched forward about 100 feet, nonchalantly sat down on the cable, stared around arrogantly, rose on one leg, then continued the crossing. As he neared the swaying middle section, the Maid-of-the-Mist, Niagara sight-seeing boat, according to prearrangement moved directly below him. Blondin lowered a rope to the deck, pulled it back up with a bottle tied to the end, took a vigorous swig, and moved on. Eighteen minutes after stepping on the rope, he landed on the Canadian side, with scarcely a hair of his flowing mane ruffled. Stopping momentarily to acknowledge the plaudits of the spectators, many too exhausted to clap loudly, he began the return trip. He seemed to fly back in exactly eight minutes.

For three summers Blondin drew paying audiences of thrill-seekers. He introduced new feats at almost every performance. He crossed the cable backwards, blindfolded, pushing a wheelbarrow, with feet fettered, at night. Once he carried a coal stove to the center of the sagging cable, cooked an omelet, and ate it. Another time he held out a top hat while a sharpshooter on the Maid-of-the-Mist shot a bullet through it. In honor of the Prince of Wales touring Canada, Blondin walked the cable on stilts. Ashen and shaky as he watched through a telescope, the Prince heaved a sigh of relief when it was over. For many years the entrance of a downtown hotel's wax museum displayed Blondin's bicycle and wheelbarrow, both with wide rims, which he used on several crossings.

A story goes that one night in a tavern Blondin overheard a man say, "I'd never let him take me over in a wheelbarrow." But another spoke up, "I would. I've watched him. He's so good. He could easily take someone over." Blondin, who had been contemplating taking someone over in his wheelbarrow, spoke up, "You're just the man I'm looking for." The man with the brave boast suddenly disappeared. He believed Blondin could safely take him over, but he wasn't willing to entrust himself to the tightrope walker. He did not believe on him—there was no committal. Later, Blondin persuaded his manager to let him be carried over and back. The experience, harrowing enough in itself, became more agonizing because gamblers had frayed some of the ropes that secured the cable. As Blondin fought to keep his balance, he shouted to his manager to make himself a dead weight and lean limply with full trust on

Blondin's back. His manager not only believed that Blondin could do it, but he committed himself fully to Blondin's care, and was safely conveyed to the other side.

To believe about Jesus is insufficient. If we believe on the Lord Jesus Christ, we shall be saved. Then we can assuredly declare, "I know Whom I have believed, and am convinced that He is able to guard what I have entrusted to Him for that day" (2 Tim. 1:12 NIV).

11

In All Four Gospels: Barabbas and the Cross

On a trip to Israel I walked down an old street in Jerusalem to a spot where the Tower of Antonio, which headquartered early Roman soldiers, reportedly once stood. Entering a building across from the Tower site, I was led below to a large pavement which had been discovered a few years previous. Often in the Holy Land, churches are erected over sacred spots. In this case, the church had been built first. Later, some workmen, repairing the church, accidentally discovered this well-preserved pavement.

Archaeologists agree that this is the pavement on which prisoners were tried before Roman governors—a corroboration of the biblical account which speaks of Pilate sitting down "in the judgment seat in a place that is called the Pavement, but in the Hebrew, Gabbatha" (John 19:13). Clearly delineated on the far end of the pavement were the markings of the "game of the kings" which soldiers played while trials were in progress. In the game, soldiers mocked the man on trial, dressing him up as a king, then

135

gambling over whether or not he would be found guilty of death, and over how soon the sentence would be carried out.

In a nearby area below the level of the pavement our guide pointed out a dungeon of several underground caves in which prisoners were held in the days of Roman rule. As I looked around, I thought of three men who possibly had been detained there, all thieves, one a murderer, and famous prisoner, and all three sentenced to death. But the most notorious of the three, Barabbas the murderer, was destined to go free.

Barabbas tossed on the dungeon floor. Any minute he expected to hear the sound of falling footsteps down the prison corridor. Momentarily he anticipated the jingle of keys, the opening of the door, the rough grasp of Roman soldiers as they led him away to mock, scourge, and crucify.

BARABBAS' GUILT

Barabbas deserved what he was getting. He was a robber and insurrectionist. Worse, he had committed murder during an uprising. He was a notable prisoner, Public Enemy Number One of Jerusalem, A.D. 30. Lagkervist, in his novel, *Barabbas*, imaginatively describes him "about thirty, powerfully built, with sallow complexion, a reddish beard and black hair. His eyebrows also black, eyes deep-set, as though wanting to hide. Under his eye a deep scar."

How does it feel to be condemned? Vividly I recall an experience several years ago as a Moody Bible Institute student on assignment at Cook County Jail in Chicago. When I finished speaking to a particular cell, someone mentioned that among the inmates in that area was a man condemned to die in the electric chair. Shaken, I asked myself, "Had I known that facing me was a man soon to die, would I have preached with more enthusiasm?" Then I thought, "Every time I face a congregation, I'm facing men, women and children all under condemnation, like Barabbas, and headed for even more certain doom."

We are all Barabbases

Few incidents are found in all four Gospels. No parable appears in all four, and only one miracle—the feeding of the 5,000. Birth accounts appear in only two Gospels. The stories of the star of Bethlehem, the wise men, the shepherds, the slaughter of babies by Herod are found in only one Gospel. Not till we come to the so-called Triumphal Entry, which began Jesus' final week leading up to the cross, do we find incidents recorded by all four. This is not surprising when we recall that His purpose on coming to earth was to die, or as He Himself put it, "not to be ministered unto, but to minister, and to give His life a ransom for many" (Matt. 20:28). Even though the cross (along with the empty tomb) is the climax toward which all four Gospels move, none of the following cross-related items occur in all four: the trial before Herod, the warning in a dream to Pilate's wife, Pilate's washing of his hands, the compelling of Simon of Cyrene to bear the cross, the crown of thorns, the repentant thief, darkness, the gambling for His robe, the ripping of the temple curtain, and the spear-thrust into Jesus' side. Of the well-known "Seven Last Sayings," six are found in only one Gospel, and the other occurs only in two.

On the other hand, many Passion episodes are related in all four: Jesus in Gethsemane, the arrest, Peter swinging his sword, Simon's denial and the cock crowing, Jesus before Caiaphas, Jesus before Pilate who delivered Him to be crucified, Jesus bearing His cross, His crucifixion at the place of a skull, the mockeries, the inscription over the cross, Jesus' loud dismissal of His spirit, and the burial by Joseph of Arimathaea.

The story of Barabbas is among those that grace all four Gospels (Matt. 27:15-26; Mark 15:6-15; Luke 23:16-25; John 18:38-40). This repetition indicates a valuable spiritual lesson. Basically, Barabbas portrays every member of the human race. Barabbas is YOU! Barabbas was in trouble. Barabbas heard good news. And that same good news is for YOU!

His name means "son of his father"

We are all sons of our father, Adam, and members of a fallen race.

He was a lawbreaker

Just as Barabbas had broken civil law, so we have broken divine law. The nature of our infraction is irrelevant, for if we violate in only one point, we are guilty of all (James 2:10).

He was an insurrectionist

We all are rebels against God. All have gone astray, each following his own self-willed way. Because children inherit Adam's nature, they tell lies early in life. They take forbidden jam, and when caught, deny their guilt with jam-smeared faces.

He was under condemnation

As certainly as Barabbas was under sentence of death and headed for execution, so we are under divine condemnation and facing a day of judgment already scheduled in God's appointment book. No one questioned the justice of his sentence. Because he was a rebel, robber, and murderer, the outraged law had laid strong hands on him. He was not awaiting trial, but execution. Like Barabbas, none of us can protest. Every mouth is stopped in the presence of a perfect law, and all stand guilty (Rom. 3:19).

He was confined

Barabbas may have been chained. At least, he was without freedom. Today multitudes are bound by habits and attitudes like alcohol, dope, sexual misconduct, and greed.

Are we really in Barabbas' class?

Perhaps we shy away from these comparisons with Barabbas, deeming him a desperate criminal and ourselves not great sinners. In one poll "91% felt they were trying to lead a good life, and 78% felt no hesitation in saying that they more than half measured up to their own standards of goodness, over 50% asserting that they were in fact following the rule of loving one's neighbor as oneself 'all the way.'" [1]

But we may be bigger sinners than we realize. A visitor approached a preacher after a series of meetings. "If I understand your preaching correctly, I've heard you say every evening that I'm a big sinner. I want you to know I'm not a big sinner. I try to do right."

The preacher replied, "Shouldn't a good person keep the commandments, especially the first and most important one?"

"What is the most important command?" asked the man.

The preacher explained that someone once asked Jesus the same question, then turning to the Gospel of Matthew, read him Jesus' answer, "Thou shalt love the Lord thy God with all thy heart, and with all thy soul, and with all thy mind" (22:37). Then the preacher asked him, "Do you keep it?"

---

1. Will Herberg, *Protestant-Catholic-Jew*, p. 86.

"No," the man answered timidly.

Then the preacher showed him the next verse, "This is the first and great commandment." Pausing, he added, "If you don't keep the first and great commandment, what does that make you?"

Meekly the man murmured, "I guess I'm a great sinner."

BARABBAS' TERROR

Barabbas knew that his execution would be soon. Two other malefactors, his pals in crime, were to die with him, but as the chief criminal and Public Enemy No. One of Jerusalem of A.D. 30, he was to have the place of eminence—the middle cross.

Though he couldn't hear the soldiers hammering away, fashioning three trees into three crosses, he couldn't keep himself from thinking of his coming ordeal. A man to be hanged has difficulty in keeping his hand away from his throat where the rope is going to choke him. A chaplain, where men were executed in the gas chamber, told how a condemned man would practice protracted breathing, even holding his breath until his eyes were bulging from their sockets. The victim knew full well, once in the chamber and the hissing sound starts, that breath he is then forcing into his lungs will be his last fresh air.

Barabbas looked at his hands. How would it feel to have both hands and feet torn by huge spikes, the wrists and joints dislocated by the downward pull of his body weight, each quivering nerve a screaming torture, suffocating because of compressed lungs, with a burning and unquenchable thirst, surrounded by a jeering crowd? Too vividly he recalled scenes of crucifixion, the slow agony of victims, sometimes lingering days.

During the night Barabbas perceived that something unusual was happening. Muffled noises, sudden outcries, tramping of feet, penetrated the thick walls. What did it all mean? Unaware that Caiaphas, the high priest, was making hasty arrangements for the trial of a self-styled Messiah, perhaps Barabbas thought they were coming earlier to take him away. Hearing the commotion, he thought his number was up. Any moment they'll be here!

Barabbas was ignorant of the drama unfolding above his dungeon in the judgment hall. Governor Pilate had a major problem on his hands. Caiaphas and his fellow-leaders had brought before him a prisoner whom they claimed was worthy of death, a sentence which required ratification by the Roman governor. But Pilate sensed the prisoner was innocent, so tried every maneuver to get Him acquitted, even sending Him to Herod on learning the prisoner came from the tetrarch's jurisdiction. Every ruse failed. Suddenly, an idea flashed into Pilate's mind. It was Passover when it was customary for the governor to release a grievous offender. If given a choice between this prisoner, Jesus, Who went about doing good, and Public Enemy No. One, Barabbas, surely the people would prefer to liberate Jesus.

Down in the dungeon Barabbas could not hear the proceedings, certainly not the question put by Pilate to the people. "Whom will ye that I release unto you? Barabbas, or Jesus which is called Christ?" But perhaps the dungeon was close enough to hear the reverberating answer as the crowd thundered, "Bar—ab—bas"!

Terrified, Barabbas pressed against the dungeon door. Why were they calling his name? What did they want with him?

He couldn't hear Pilate's next question, "What shall I do with Jesus?" Perhaps he could hear them yell in reply, "Let Him be crucified!"

His blood chilled. He had heard his name, "Bar—ab—bas," followed by "Let Him be crucified!" He thought they were clamoring for his immediate death.

BARABBAS' FREEDOM

His fears were soon confirmed. The sound of footsteps echoed down the dungeon hall. Keys jingled. The door rattled on its hinges. In stepped Roman soldiers. But they just stood at the open door. They did not grab him. Instead, the centurion barked, "You may go."

"They're mocking me," Barabbas thought. "They just want to add to my torment."

The soldiers pointed to the door.

"But," protested the condemned man.

"Out!" the soldiers repeated, again pointing to the door.

Hardly able to believe them, Barabbas walked out a free man. He pinched himself a few times to make sure he wasn't dreaming.

Matthew simply says, "Then released he Barabbas unto them, and when he had scourged Jesus, he delivered Him to be crucified." Mark, Luke, and John record the incident in almost identical words.

Later that morning Barabbas undoubtedly joined the throng on the hill outside the city wall. Feeling some sense of shame, he hesitated on the fringe of the crowd. He looked up at the three crosses. Concentrating on the cross on the right, he recognized the victim. He was his pal in thievery—they had been in prison together. Then he gazed at the cross on the left. He, too, had been in the dungeon cell.

Then Barabbas looked at the middle cross. He didn't recognize that victim. But he vaguely recalled hearing His name. He turned to a stranger nearby, "Who's that on the middle cross?"

With a look of amazement the stranger replied, "You don't know who He is? Why, I used to be a leper. I had to live outside my village and cry, 'Unclean, unclean.' I couldn't go home to my wife, nor take my children on my lap, nor would anyone employ me. But one day that man came along and touched me. And I was immediately healed. Now I live at home with my wife and children, and have my old job back!"

Overhearing the conversation, another bystander turned to Barabbas, "You really don't know who He is?" Without waiting for an answer, the man continued, "I was born blind. I never saw a sunset nor my mother's face till one day He came along and touched my eyes. Ever since then I've seen!"

Now Barabbas was sure. It was Jesus on that cross! But everything He had heard about Jesus was good. They said He went about healing, teaching, comforting, helping. Staring at the center tree, Barabbas shuddered, "I should be up there. I should be on that cross! The nails should be in MY hands! The crowds should be gaping at ME! It should be MY blood dripping to the ground! I'm the criminal! HE's innocent!" The title of a modern gospel song describes what must have been Barabbas' mood, "I should have been crucified."

Dr. C. I. Scofield suggested that "Barabbas had no need to be a theologian to form a good working theory of the atonement. First, he knew that he was a guilty wretch, under the righteous condemnation of the law.

"Secondly, Barabbas knew that the Sufferer before him had done no sin.

"Thirdly, he knew that Jesus was, for him, a true substitute. He was verily and actually dying in his place. . . . Whoever, in the coming ages, might question whether Christ's death was vicarious and substitutional, he could never question it.

"Fourthly, he knew that he had done nothing to merit the mar-

velous interposition of that substitutional death. Whatever may have
been back of it, it reached him as an act of pure grace.

"Fifthly, he knew that Christ's death for him was perfectly effica-
cious. There was, therefore, nothing for him to add to it. Just
because Christ was dying, he was living."

Scofield concluded his remarks with a quote, "John McNeill, the
great Scotch preacher, well says, 'My brethren, let me commend to
you Barabbas' theory of the atonement. It is a good theory to
preach on, pray on, sing on, die on.'" [2]

Had Isaac Watts' hymn been written, Barabbas could have para-
phrased it,

> Alas, and does my Savior bleed?
> And does my Sovereign die?
> Does He devote that sacred head
> For such a worm as I?
>
> It is for crimes that I have done
> He groans upon the tree.
> Amazing pity! Grace unknown!
> And love beyond degree!

As darkness settled over the scene, he could have sung,

> Well might the sun in darkness hide,
> And shut its glories in,
> While Christ, the Mighty Maker, dies
> For man the creature's sin.

No one knows if Barabbas understood the theological ramifications of the situation. One legend does say that sometime during
the blackness of those hours he ran to the foot of the cross, fell
prostrate, then lifting his head and beating upon his chest, cried
out, "O Thou, Jesus of Nazareth, I don't know much about you.
But this I know. You are hanging there in my place." If Barabbas,
like the repentant thief, caught a glimpse of the saving power of
Christ and threw himself on His mercy, he will be in heaven.

"A murderer in heaven?" someone objects. Yes! Remarkably,
sizable portions of the Bible were written by murderers. Moses,
who one day killed an Egyptian and hid his body in the sand, wrote
the first five books, Genesis through Deuteronomy. David, sweet

---

2. Tract, *Barabbas Goes Free*, Book Fellowship, North Syracuse, N.Y.

singer of Israel, who committed adultery with Bathsheba and then engineered the death of her husband, Uriah, penned about half the Psalms, including the lovely twenty-third. The apostle Paul, who spearheaded Stephen's martyrdom, breathed out threatenings and slaughter against the early church, and voted for the death of many saints (Acts 26:10), wrote approximately half the books of the New Testament, and carried the gospel all over the Roman Empire as God's chosen apostle to the Gentiles. Jesus died on the cross for every kind of sinner, even murderers.

Because Jesus died in his place, Barabbas went free, no more to worry about courts, judges, prisoners, nor jailers. He could not be charged with his previous crime. All the murderer's chains, curse, penalty and disgrace were transferred to Jesus Christ. No judicial procedure could be instituted against him.

His pardoned condition in a way pictures the doctrine of justification. Justification is the legal act of God whereby, on account of the merit of Christ, the sinner is declared no longer exposed to the terror of breaking God's divine law, but stands before God acquitted. It is not the inner making of the sinner righteous, which involves regeneration and sanctification, but rather the objective, judicial declaration by God from outside the person that the sinner is now righteous.

Commenting on Barabbas, Donald Grey Barnhouse wrote, "He was the only man in the world who could say that Jesus Christ took his physical place. But I can say Jesus Christ took my spiritual place. . . . It was I who deserved that the wrath of God should be poured out on me. I deserved the eternal punishment of the lake of fire. . . . He was handed over to judgment because of my sins. . . . He was satisfying the debt of divine justice and holiness. That is why I say that Christianity can be expressed in the three phrases: I deserved hell; Jesus took my hell; there is nothing left for me but heaven." [3]

BARABBAS' ACCEPTANCE

Suppose Barabbas had refused the good tidings brought by the soldiers. What if he had said, "I'll stay here till I can prove myself a good man worthy of release. I'll become a good citizen first, then think of going free"? He would have died in prison. But

3. *Our Daily Bread*, Radio Bible Class Publications, Grand Rapids, MI, March 30, 1988.

Barabbas was freed, not because he could ever make himself good, but because, though he was bad, Jesus died in his place. He did nothing, nor could do anything, to deserve the delight of deliverance.

For twentieth-century Barabbases the message is the same. Although rebellious lawbreakers, under divine sentence, we may go free, not because we are good, but because Jesus died in our place. We cannot earn freedom. We need a Savior. Jesus is that Savior Who releases us from condemnation by His suffering on the cross, then enables us to go out and be good.

Had Barabbas refused the offer of liberation, he would have insulted those bearing the good news, shown ingratitude, and perhaps had the door closed in his face to await execution at a later date. How foolish he would have been.

In 1830 a man named George Wilson, found guilty of train robbery and putting a man's life in jeopardy, was sentenced to die. President Andrew Jackson extended a pardon to the condemned criminal awaiting execution in a penitentiary. For some reason Wilson refused the pardon. Prison officials proceeded with execution plans till Wilson's lawyers obtained a stay, contending that a pardoned man could not be hanged. The case went to the Supreme Court which ruled, "A pardon is a deed to the validity of which delivery is essential; and delivery is not complete without acceptance; it may then be rejected by the person to whom it is tendered; and if it rejected, we have discovered no power in a court to force it on him. It may be supposed, that no being condemned to death would reject a pardon, but the rule must be the same in capital cases and misdemeanors." [4]

Though carefully reading the pages of material on this case, I could find no mention of whether or not George Wilson was ever executed. But if he did hang, how foolish to turn down a pardon. Barabbas, when the sheer wonder of it all finally broke through, received the message with rapture, shook off his chains, left the dungeon, and walked out a free man to inhale the fresh air of springtime and to contemplate the beauty of the boundless sky.

Today, all who, like Barabbas, languish in the gloomy dungeon

---

4. Case No. 150 in *Reports of Cases Argued and Adjudged in the Supreme Court of the United States*, January Term 1883, by Richard Peters, Vol. VII, third edition, Banks & Brothers, Law Publishers, New York, 1884, p. 95.

of guilt, bound by chains of evil habits, headed for a Christless eternity, need only to visit Calvary, and say with the hymnwriter, Elizabeth C. Clephane,

> Upon the cross of Jesus
> Mine eyes at times can see
> The very dying form of One
> Who suffered there for me;
> And from my smitten heart with tears,
> Two wonders I confess—
> The wonders of His glorious love
> And my unworthiness.

Because Jesus took our place, we may go free, uncondemned, to live in peace, joy, and newness of life.

12

In All Four Gospels: The Empty Tomb

Thomas Jefferson, President of the United States and a man of wide interests, made a revision of the four Gospels. Omitting every reference to both the miracles and deity of Jesus, he cut verse by verse out of a printed Bible, and pasted his excerpts into a 46-page book which he titled, *The Life and Morals of Jesus of Nazareth*. Deliberately he deleted every reference to the resurrection, reworking the Gospel accounts to give us an abbreviated, emasculated, anemic Jesus, seemingly "totally human and quite dead."

Jefferson left out the most exciting part of the Gospels. The empty tomb, the startling angelic announcement, "He is risen," and the many electrifying appearances of the risen Lord made that first Easter the most dramatic day of His entire ministry. All four Gospels devote their final chapters to this climactic event (Matt. 28, Mark 16, Luke 24, John 20, 21).

In the early dawn the forms of several women could be seen wending their way toward the sepulcher where Jesus had been hurriedly buried. They intended to anoint His body properly, a minis-

147

tration which the arrival of the Sabbath had denied them. The gloom of the early morn matched their mood. But beneath their melancholy were hearts of undying devotion.

What love! Last at the cross; first at the tomb!

What courage! To think of entering a tomb sealed by Roman authority and guarded by Roman soldiers!

What faith! How could they move the stone? Tombs were often hollowed out of rock and covered by a large, circular stone, adequate barrier against vandals and animals. Sometimes a ton in weight, this stone would require the effort of several muscular men to move it.

To their amazement the women found the stone rolled away, and a guard who exclaimed, "He is not here: for He is risen, as He said. Come see the place where the Lord lay" (Matt. 28:6). After looking into the grave, the women hurried to tell the disciples. At first the message sounded like an idle tale, but the disciples ran to the tomb and found it empty. The hours that followed were filled with per-plexing reports of Jesus' appearances, the last one that day to His followers in the upper room. Finally, the glorious truth overcame their unbelief. Tears turned to triumph! Jesus had indeed risen!

THE LITERALNESS OF THE EMPTY TOMB

Some who speak of the resurrection do not mean that He rose bodily. Engaging in mental gymnastics, they claim it was His influ-ence that came out of the grave, not His body. Hearing a pastor so refer to the resurrection, a congregation may not realize that he does not believe in a literal resurrection. To such a pastor, Jesus' body never emerged from the tomb—it was His spirit that rose.

To deny that the body of Christ rose, while at the same time affirming His resurrection, sounds like double-talk and smacks of intellectual dishonesty. This verbal gobbledygook reminds of the thief in Illinois who over a weekend stole hundreds of pairs of shoes from a store, but left the boxes in place on the shelves. On Monday, when clerks went hunting for sizes, they found the boxes but no shoes. Theological thieves preserve the term, "resurrection of Christ," while robbing it of its real meaning.

Someone imagined this conversation, "Pastor, do you believe in the resurrection of Jesus?"

"Of course, I do. Yes, I am a believer."

"It's great to hear you say that, Pastor. Some claim you're not a believer because you do not believe that Jesus rose from the grave."

"Of course, I don't believe that Jesus literally rose from the grave."

"But I thought you said you believed in the resurrection."

"Yes, I do, but the resurrection means the rise of faith in the minds of the disciples as a result of Jesus' death on the cross."

"Oh, then you don't really believe in the resurrection."

"Yes, of course I do."

Such dialogue is theological equivocation. The four Gospels plainly assert Jesus' literal resurrection. Except for the graveclothes, the tomb was empty and His body risen. To His frightened disciples He showed Himself alive with many infallible proofs. On the first Easter night in the Upper Room, pointing to the nail marks in His hands and His feet, He said, "Behold My hands and My feet, that it is I Myself" (Luke 24:39, 40). Absent Thomas skeptically declared that he would not believe until he examined those nail prints. A week later Thomas was invited to reach his finger into Jesus' hands and to put his hand into Jesus' side. Completely convinced, Thomas exclaimed in worship, "My Lord and my God" (John 20:28).

Eleven appearances are recorded during Jesus' forty-day stay on earth before the Ascension. Accounts, which seem contradictory, in reality may be complementary. Admittedly, harmonization has its problems, but here is an attempt.

1. To Mary, who reached the tomb after Peter and John left it (Mark 16:9; John 20:11-18);
2. To the women after leaving the tomb (Matt. 28:9, 10);
3. To Peter (Luke 24:34; 1 Cor. 15:5);
4. To the two on the Emmaus road (Luke 24:13-35);
5. To the ten disciples and others, minus Thomas (Luke 24:33-45; John 20:19-23);
6. To the eleven, including Thomas (John 20:24-29);
7. To several disciples fishing on Galilee (John 21);
8. To the disciples on a Galilean mount (Matt. 28:16-20);
9. To 500 brethren at once (1 Cor. 15:6);
10. To James (1 Cor. 15:7);
11. To the disciples at the Ascension (Mark 16:19; Luke 24:50-52; Acts 1:9-11).

As the Apostles' Creed says, "the third day He rose again from the dead." It was His body that rose, not His influence, just as it wasn't His influence that later ascended into heaven. Nor was it

His influence that sits at the right hand of God. Nor is it His influence that some day will come back to earth to judge the quick and the dead.

THE PROMINENCE OF THE EMPTY TOMB

From first to finish the Bible gives prominence to the resurrection of Jesus.

Prophesied in the Old Testament

In the Upper Room that first Easter night the Lord Jesus gave His astonished disciples what must have been the finest survey course in Old Testament prophecy. He explained how many Scriptures "written in the law of Moses, and in the prophets, and in the psalms" were fulfilled in His death and resurrection (Luke 24:44, 45). This teaching session was the source of many Old Testament references which the apostles later claimed as predicting the resurrection. It's likely that in that Easter-night meeting Jesus included the following examples.

Law Abraham's near-sacrifice of Isaac prefigured the resurrection. For three days after God's command to offer up Isaac, Abraham considered his beloved son as good as dead. When the divine voice ordered Abraham not to plunge the poised knife into Isaac's bound body, Abraham received his son back from the dead figuratively, anticipating the third-day resurrection of God's beloved Son (Heb. 11:17-19).

Prophets Jesus had earlier cited Jonah's three-day stay inside the fish as a type of His own burial in the heart of the earth (Matt. 12:40).

Psalms In his Pentecost sermon, as proof of the resurrection, Peter later quoted from a Psalm, "neither wilt Thou suffer Thine Holy One to see corruption" (Ps. 16:10; Acts 2:27). Paul used the same Psalm for the same purpose (Acts 13:35).

Predicted by Jesus in the Gospels

After Peter's confession of Christ's deity, the Lord repeatedly foretold His inevitable sufferings, death and rising "again the third day" (Matt. 16:21; 17:22, 23; 20:18, 19). After His transfiguration Christ charged Peter, James, and John to tell no one of the vision "until the Son of man be risen again from the dead" (17:9).

Proclaimed by the Apostles

Acts The climax of Peter's Pentecost sermon was the resurrection, "This Jesus hath God raised up, whereof we all are witnesses" (2:32). A dozen major messages in Acts culminate in the resurrection. Paul's sermon on Mars Hill was disrupted when he reached the resurrection (17:31, 32).

Epistles The empty tomb undergirds Christian doctrine throughout the epistles. Paul devotes a long chapter to the theme (1 Cor. 15). Peter said we have been given a living hope by the resurrection of Jesus Christ from the dead (1 Pet. 1:3).

Revelation John, who penned the last book of the Bible, begins with an awesome vision of Christ Who declares, "I am He that liveth, and was dead; and, behold, I am alive for evermore, Amen; and have the keys of hell and of death" (Rev. 1:18).

The empty tomb is integrally woven into the fabric of Scripture. A man declared his intent to found a new religion that would outshine Christianity. Came this retort, "There's one thing you must do. You must permit yourself to be crucified, and then you must rise again from the dead."

ATTEMPTS AT EXPLAINING THE EMPTY TOMB

Some skeptics put the resurrection in the same class as folklore. I have in my files a letter written by a professor of New Testament Interpretation in one of our midwest seminaries in which he says that he cannot defend the literal rising of Christ's body any more than he can explain the flight of Santa Claus from the north pole and his descent down chimneys with his pack of toys. But the four Gospels report an empty grave as fact, not fanciful, fictitious legend. How do skeptics account for that empty tomb?

Wrong tomb

Some say that Jesus' followers went to the wrong tomb. But this suggestion raises serious questions. We usually find the grave of a loved one with relative ease, even though surrounded by other tombstones. How could the disciples have been mistaken when this was likely the only sepulcher in Joseph's garden? Why did every group go to the wrong tomb, especially the women who had watched Jesus buried in that tomb? How did the angels know that the disciples were going to a wrong tomb, and to which wrong tomb? How did the grave clothes arrive there?

Swoon theory

Some theorize that Jesus didn't die but merely fainted. Later the cool, damp air of the sepulcher revived Him. Seeing Him again, the disciples labored under the delusion that He had actually died and was back from the dead. This idea was popularized in a book, *The Passover Plot*.

How could Roman soldiers, so accustomed to the task of crucifixion, be easily deceived? These experienced observers could tell when a victim had expired. They did not break His legs to hasten death, as they did with the thieves, because they knew He had already breathed His last. Also, official government pronouncement after specific investigation ordered by Pilate, who was surprised at Jesus' soon death, declared Him deceased. Obvious purpose of the women coming to the tomb was to anoint a corpse, not a comatose. How could someone, so severely debilitated by unimaginable agony, and without food and water for so many hours, push back a stone which required several men to move? How could He walk normally many miles to Emmaus? Why did He appear in majestic power instead of as a sick weakling?

Subjective vision

Some argue that the fervency with which the disciples wished Jesus back from the dead made them imagine they saw Him alive.

In answer, we cannot bring back the dead by merely wishing them alive. How could such visions arise when the disciples did not expect Him to rise? The fact is—reports of His resurrection fell on their ears like idle tales. How could these visions begin as early as the third day when they were still downhearted? How does the same subjective vision or hallucination come to 500 persons simultaneously? Rarely do even two people ever have the same dream at the same time. In reality, the disciples were unbelievers at first. They doubted that we might believe.

Telegraph theory

Some say that God sent the disciples an objective vision of the risen Christ, though actually He had not risen from the grave, to motivate them to fulfill the Great Commission.

This would mean that God deceived the apostles. But God does not promote His work by trickery, especially His plan of building His church in this age. Since this view admits the supernatural in a limited degree, why not accept the full miracle of the resurrection?

Lettuce theory

Mentioned by Tertullian in the second century, this hypothesis proposes that the gardener, irritated by visitors that Easter morning who trampled on his recently planted lettuce seedlings near the tomb, reburied the body elsewhere.

Had the gardener removed the body, he could easily have squelched the "rumor" of the resurrection by producing the body.

Twin brother theory

This speculates that Jesus had a twin brother who stayed out of sight during Jesus' ministry, but who revealed himself the Sunday after the crucifixion, leading people to believe that Jesus had returned from the grave.

Ludicrous as the Lettuce and Twin brother theories may seem, they were proposed by intelligent people unable to accept the miracle of the resurrection.

Theft theory

Someone stole the body, so this conjecture goes. But who? Not the leaders of the nation, for this is exactly what they did not want to happen. Recalling Jesus' statement that He would rise after three days, they requested a guard "until the third day, lest His disciples come by night, and steal Him away, and say unto the people, He is risen from the dead: so the last error shall be worse than the first" (Matt. 27:64).

Nor did the guards steal the corpse. Their duty was to guard it. How lame their excuse, "His disciples came by night, and stole Him away while we slept" (Matt. 28:13). If asleep, how did they know what happened? A witness, testifying as to what he saw while asleep, would carry no weight in a court of law.

Falsehood theory

A popular explanation claims the disciples stole Jesus' body, buried it elsewhere, then preached that He had risen from the grave. For the disciples to have done so would characterize them, some of

154   *The Four Faces of Jesus*

whom penned New Testament books, not merely mistaken witnesses, but unmitigated liars. The superstructure of almost twenty
centuries of the Christian church has then been built on a flimsy
fabrication. The perpetrators of such willful imposture would be
considered knaves, not honored apostles.

Chuck Colson says in *Kingdoms in Conflict*, "In my Watergate
experience I saw the inability of men—powerful, highly motivated
professionals—to hold together a conspiracy based on a lie. It was
less than three weeks from the time that Mr. Nixon knew all the
facts to the time that John Dean went to the prosecutors. . . . The
actual cover-up lasted less than a month. Yet Christ's powerless
followers maintained to their grim deaths by execution that they
had in fact seen Jesus Christ raised from the dead. There was no
conspiracy, no Passover plot. Men and women do not give up their
comfort—and certainly not their lives—for what they know to be a
lie." [1]

The falsehood theory poses a major psychological problem. What
explains the sudden change from cowardice to courage on the part
of the disciples? Peter, who had denied the Lord in front of a maid,
stands before thousands of people fifty days later, fearlessly flinging
out the charge, "Him, . . . ye have taken, and by wicked hands have
crucified and slain" (Acts 2:23). The disciples, who in Gethsemane
had forsaken Jesus and fled, a few weeks later boldly face the same
Sanhedrin which had condemned their Master, and though commanded not to speak Jesus' name, daily "ceased not to teach and
preach Jesus Christ" (5:42).

Only their unshaken conviction in the resurrection can account
for their willingness to suffer beatings, prison, and the martyrdoms
which ended the lives of most, if not all, of the apostles. They had
seen One Who, though buried in a tomb, had emerged triumphantly alive, conqueror of death! Because He possessed the keys of
death, they too would live after death.

The foreword of an eighteenth century book tells of two educat-
ed men who, persuaded that the Bible was an imposture, determined to expose the cheat by attacking what they considered the
two bulwarks of Christianity: the resurrection of Christ and the
conversion of Paul. Lord Lyttleton, Oxford graduate and member
of Parliament, who lived on intimate terms with Bolingbroke, Pope,

1. Zondervan, 1987, p. 70.

Chesterfield and Dr. Samuel Johnson, chose the conversion of Paul as his topic of hostile criticism. His friend, Gilbert West, took the resurrection of Christ. Neither had read to any extent in the New Testament, so in fairness to their assignment began to examine the evidence. The foreword gives the outcome: "Both sat down to their respective tasks full of prejudice, but the result of their separate attempts was that they were both converted by their efforts to overthrow the truth of Christianity. They came together not as they expected, to exult over an imposture exposed to ridicule, but to lament over their own folly, and to felicitate each other on their joint conviction that the Bible was the word of God. Their able inquiries have furnished two of the most valuable treatises in favor of revelation, one entitled, *'Observations on the Conversion of St. Paul'*, and the other *'Observations on the Resurrection of Christ.'*" [2]

A more recent volume, *Who Moved the Stone?*, was penned by an English lawyer who originally meant to disprove the resurrection. But compelled by his investigation to write in defense of the empty tomb, he titled the first chapter, "The Book That Refused to Be Written." [3]

THE SIGNIFICANCE OF THE EMPTY TOMB

English preacher R. W. Dale was preparing an Easter sermon when the truth of Christ's resurrection burst in upon him with striking power. "Christ is alive," he exclaimed loudly. He began walking around his study repeating, "He is alive. Christ is alive— alive!" Not only for Easter, but for months afterward he delighted in the theme of the risen Christ. He started the custom of having a resurrection hymn sung every Sunday morning to remind the congregation that they were worshiping a living Christ. [4]

Vital implications flow from the resurrection truth.

Jesus proved Himself everything He claimed to be

Repeatedly Jesus predicted He would come back from the dead. Failure to rise would have thrown doubt on all His claims. But by rising He was "declared to be the Son of God with power" (Rom. 1:4). Others have claimed they would return from the dead and

---

2. Lord Lyttleton, *The Conversion of St. Paul*, American Tract Society, no date.
3. Frank Morison, Faber and Faber, London, 1958.
4. Warren Wiersbe, *Walking with the Giants*, p. 45.

communicate with the living, but never have. No one expects an ordinary man to come back from the grave. But Jesus was extraordinary in His birth, teachings, miracles, purity, death and resurrection. His rising fits His supernatural character.

When some years ago reports spread that Buddha's bones had been discovered, the people of India lined the streets of Bombay to pay homage. A missionary, noting their prostrations, commented to a fellow-missionary, "If they could find one bone of Jesus Christ, Christianity would fall to pieces!"

Jesus is victor over death

Death is a terrible enemy, plays no favorites, has a key to every home, cares not for our plans, sometimes beckons the young before the old and the strong before the weak, and ultimately calls with an appointment we all must keep. A funeral hearse in Connecticut bore this ominous license plate, "U-2."

But Christ abolished the power of death (2 Tim. 1:10). Knowing its full power, He permitted His body to become a corpse and to be buried in a tomb. Then He seized the keys of death. A new exclamation broke the air, "He is risen!" Alive in His crucified body, He exclaimed, "I am He that liveth, and was dead, and behold, I am alive for evermore" (Rev. 1:18).

Dr. Donald Grey Barnhouse was driving his children to his wife's funeral service. At a stoplight they found themselves beside a huge truck, which cast a shadow across the neighboring field. As the shadow loomed large, Barnhouse said, "Children, look at that truck, and look at its shadow. Which would you rather be run over by— the truck or its shadow?" His youngest child spoke up. "The shadow. It couldn't hurt anybody." Agreeing, Barnhouse added, "Death is a truck, but the shadow is all that ever touches the Christian. The truck ran over the Lord Jesus. Only the shadow passed over mother."

Jesus' victory over death makes possible the Psalmist's word, "Though I walk through the valley of the shadow of death, I will fear no evil" (23:4). Though death may come to the believer, its sting has been removed.

The truth of the resurrection can penetrate the armor of atheism. George Bush reported an amazing incident at the funeral of Soviet leader Brezhnev. The ceremony ran with military precision. Coldness pervaded the event—marching soldiers, steel helmets,

Marxist rhetoric, without prayers or hymns or mention of God. He said, "I happened to be in just the right spot to see Mrs. Brezhnev. She walked up, took one last look at her husband and there—in the cold, gray center of that totalitarian state, she traced the sign of the cross over her husband's chest. I was stunned. In that simple act, God had broken through the core of the Communist system." [5]

Jesus has the power to raise others

Christ vacating the sepulcher dominates the Easter message, overshadowing an incident recorded only in Matthew, "Many bodies of the saints which slept arose, And came out of the graves after His resurrection, and went into the holy city, and appeared unto many" (27:52, 53). Because of His empty tomb, there were other empty tombs. What a hair-raising shock for anyone in the vicinity that morning to see people, long since buried, crawl from their tombs, stand erect, then head homeward.

Though limited in location and number, the miracle graphically prefigured what Christ will some day do. Every grave the world round will be opened, not just those of saints near Jerusalem, and every body will come forth, sinners to judgment and saints to life. These empty tombs rehearsed in miniature that momentous resurrection event yet future.

Jesus' atonement was acceptable to His heavenly Father

In some eastern countries, when a buyer places the purchase price down on a merchant's table, it is customary for the seller to raise his hand to signify his acceptance of that price. Jesus laid down His life to pay the price for our redemption. Three days later the Father lifted Jesus up from the grave to indicate His acceptance of that price. Jesus has successfully paid it all. Paul put it, He "was delivered for our offences, and was raised again for our justification" (Rom. 4:25).

Jesus Christ will be the judge some day

Judgment is certain. As surely as Independence Day falls on July 4th, and Christmas on December 25, so judgment will fall on the exact day already scheduled on the divine calendar. Paul wrote that God had set a day "when He will judge the world with justice by

---

5. *Washington Post*, July 18, 1987.

the man He has appointed." Paul leaves no doubt as to identity of that judge, for he adds, "He has given proof of this to all men by raising Him from the dead" (Acts 17:31 NIV).

Jesus made the same resurrection power available to us

A neglected Easter truth declares that the same power that raised Jesus from the tomb is available to help us gain victory in our Christian lives. Paul prayed that believers would come to know "His incomparably great power . . . which He exerted in Christ when He raised Him from the dead and seated Him at His right hand in the heavenly realms" (Eph. 1:19, 20 NIV).

Paul says it is this same power that raises the spiritually dead and gives newness of life to those dead in sin (2:1). That same power is at the disposal of believers for victory over temptation, strength in adversity, and growth in Christlikeness.

Jesus Christ gives hope

I'll never forget the first funeral I conducted—in fact, it was the first Protestant funeral I ever attended. Just 21 years of age, I had been sent out by Moody Bible Institute's Practical Work Department to conduct the funeral of a 24-year-old Mexican mother with no church connection. She was survived by a bewildered husband and four little children. Also present, and most emotional of all, was the girl's mother, who just before the casket was closed at the end of the service, let out a blood-curdling scream, "Never see her again!" I can still hear her cry of utter hopelessness, which she repeated over and over.

A boy, living in Idaho, could never forget a lumber buyer named Benham who stayed a week in his parents' home. An outspoken atheist, Benham could repeat persuasively the major arguments for atheism. He boasted that he spent most of his money and time proving God did not exist. Irrevocably he held there was no after-life, no heaven, and no hell. Twenty years later, the boy grown to manhood, attending a convention in St. Paul, Minnesota, noticed Mr. Benham, who recalling the youth, invited him to lunch.

It became immediately evident that the atheist had lost his poise. He acted like a man facing a death sentence. Now 71, Benham explained that he had an incurable blood disease and less than six months to live. Then he launched into an incident about an elderly lady who lay at death's door in a hospital where Benham had gone for a check-up. There a nurse enlisted him as a witness to the will of a dying woman who could not sign because of a paralyzed arm. Entering the lady's room, he was mesmerized by the utter serenity of this woman who was facing the end with a smiling countenance. The nurse scribbled the stricken woman's instructions. When all the witnesses had signed the will, the lady smiled, thanked them, and said, "And now I am ready to leave this pain-racked body to meet my Maker, my husband, my father, my mother, and all my friends who have gone before me. Won't that be wonderful!"

Tears started down Benham's pale, wrinkled cheeks. "Look at me," he whispered hoarsely. "I've lain awake every night since learning my days were numbered, staring at the ceiling with nothing to look forward to—except my life ending in a handful of ashes. That's the difference between me, an atheist, and that lady. She, a believer, faces her final days with a smile. Here am I, an unbeliever, with every moment a nightmare, facing nothing but a cold tomb." Then he added, "I would shove my hands into a bed of red-hot coals if by so doing I could secure a belief in a Supreme Being and an afterlife!"

That lady demonstrated the rightful possession of every person who trusts in the Savior—"a living hope through the resurrection of Jesus Christ from the dead" (1 Pet. 1:3 NIV).

A FINAL THOUGHT

The final chapters of the four Gospels seem to point progressively toward epochal events in the ministry of Jesus.

- The last chapter of Matthew records His RESURRECTION.
- Mark's final section refers to His ASCENSION (16:19).
- Luke's closing remarks include mention of His SENDING OF THE HOLY SPIRIT (24:49).
- John's last conversation points to the SECOND COMING OF CHRIST (21:21-23).

In the meantime let's ask ourselves these questions:

- Is Jesus KING of my life?
- Do I show the SERVANT spirit?
- Do I reflect the tenderness of the Son of MAN?
- Is He my GOD? Have I placed my faith in Him as my Savior, and have I enthroned Him as my Lord, keeping myself from all the idols that vie for my worship?

Bibliography

Barnhouse, Donald Grey. *Mark: The Servant Gospel*, Victor Books, 1988.

_____. *Our Daily Bread*, Radio Bible Class Publications, Grand Rapids, MI, March 30, 1988.

Bush, George. Quoted in the *Washington Post*, July 18, 1987.

Clark, Gordon H. Martin, Clark, Clarke, and Ruddick, *A History of Philosophy*, F. S. Crofts Co., 1941, p. 241.

Colson, Charles. *Kingdoms in Conflict*, Zondervan, 1987, p. 70.

Drury, Bill. Teen Haven, PO Box 31, Willow Street, PA, 17584.

Edwards, James. "The Calling," in *Christianity Today*, February 5, 1988, p. 66.

Eerdman, Charles. *The Gospel of Matthew*, Westminster Press, 1920, Foreword.

Greenleaf, Robert K. *Servant Leadership*, Ramsey, NJ: Paulist Press, 1977.

_____. *The Servant as Religious Leader*, Peterborough, NH: Windy Row Press, 1982.

Gregory, Daniel S. *Why Four Gospels?*, Bible League Book Co., 1907, pp. 14, 255.

Grounds, Vernon. *Seminary Studies Series*, published by Denver Conservative Baptist Seminary, Denver, CO.

Herberg, Will. *Protestant, Catholic, Jew*, University of Chicago Press, 1983, p. 86.

Hope, Ginger. "Gold Mine in a Dumpster" in *World Vision*, August-September, 1991, p. 16.

Howard, Fred. *New York Times*, in Book Review section, July 2, 1989, a review of *Men from Earth*, by Buzz Aldrin and Malcolm McConnell.

Hughes, Kent and Barbara. *Liberating Ministry from the Success Syndrome*, Tyndale, 1987, p. 45.

"In Boston, a Busing Plan That Works," in *Newsweek*, March 6, 1989, p. 27.

Ironside, Harry A. *Addresses on Luke*, Loizeaux Brothers, 1947, p. 629.

Johnson, Alan. "'Fulfilled Jews' or 'Former Jews'?" in *Christianity Today*, October 7, 1988, p. 68.

Jukes, Andrew John. *The Characteristic Differences of the Four Gospels*, London, J. Nisbet & Co., 1882.

Lagerkvist, Par. *Barabbas*, Random, 1955.

Larson, Erik. "To Have and to Hold, Product Advertisers Need Perfect Hands," in *Wall Street Journal*, May 14, 1987.

Little, Paul. *How to Give Away Your Faith*, Intervarsity Press, 1966, pp. 106, 124, 125.

Lyttleton, Lord. *The Conversion of St. Paul*, American Tract Society, Foreword, no date, but published in 18th century.

Martin, Walter. *The Agony of Deceit*, edited by Michael Horton, Moody Press, 1990, p. 92.

McQuilkin, Robert. "Living by Vows" in *Christianity Today*, October 8, 1990, pp. 38-40.

Morgan, G. Campbell. *The Gospel According to Luke*, New York: Revell, 1939, p. 277.

Medicine section, "Making TLC a Requirement" in *Newsweek*, August 12, 1991, p. 56*ff.*

Nelson, Lawrence E. *Our Roving Bible*, Abingdon-Cokesbury, 1945, pp. 152-154.

Peters, Richard. Case No. 150 in *Reports of Cases Argued and Adjudged in the Supreme Court of the United States*, January Term 1883, Vol. VII, third edition, Banks & Brothers, Law Publishers, New York, 1884, p. 95.

Pink, A. W. *Why Four Gospels?*, Reiner Publications, Swengel Publications, 1921.

Pippert, Wesley G. *An Ethics of News*, Georgetown University Press, 1989, p. 24.

Pulpit Commentary, Genesis, p. 441, Funk & Wagnalls Co., new edition, no date.

Robertson, A. T. *Harmony of the Gospels*, Harper and Brothers, 1922, p. 61.

_____. *Studies in Mark's Gospel*, Macmillan, 1919, p. 24.

Soltau, George. *Four Portraits of the Lord Jesus Christ*, Charles C. Cook, New York, NY, 1905.

Scofield, C. I. Tract, *Barabbas Goes Free*, Book Fellowship, North Syracuse, NY, no date.

_____. Quoted by George Soltau in *Four Portraits of the Lord Jesus Christ*, Charles C. Cook, New York, NY, *Foreword*, 1905.

Stott, John. *Life in Christ*, Tyndale, 1991, p. 25.

Street, R. Alan. *The Effective Invitation*, Revell, 1984, pp. 181, 182.

Taylor, Vincent. *The Gospels—A Short Introduction*, London: The Epworth Press, no date, pp. 39, 60.

Tenney, Merrill C. *The Genius of the Gospels*, Eerdmans, 1951 pp. 54, 81, 82.

_____. *The Gospel of Belief,* Eerdmans, 1948, p. 33.

Van Valkenburgh, F. D. *Why Four Gospels,* Pentecostal Publishing Co., Louisville, KY, 1918, p. 55.

Waddell, Genevieve J., article, "Jose!" by Jose Pagan as told to Genevieve J. Waddell, in *Decision,* June 1973.

War Cry, published by Salvation Army, Nov. 21, 1987, and February 27, 1988.

Wierick, John. "The Profit Prophet" in *World Vision* magazine, December 1988-January 1989, p. 21.

Wiersbe, Warren. *Walking with the Giants,* Baker, 1976, p. 45.

Wolkomir, Richard. "The Best Criticism I Ever Received," in *Reader's Digest,* July 1986, p. 134ff.

Yancey, Philip. "Low Pay, Long Hours, No Applause," in *Christianity Today,* Nov. 18, 1988, p. 80.

Scripture Index

Discussion Guide

1. Four Views of the Good News

1. On page 12, Dr. Flynn says that the four evangelists (Matthew, Mark, Luke & John) ". . . did not set out to give a biographical sketch of the Lord Jesus." Think about that statement and discuss.

2. Read and discuss the question on page 13, "Would it not have been simpler if we had been given one . . . account of Jesus' life . . .?"

3. On page 17, Dr. Flynn says, "As a building may be viewed from four different sides, so the Holy Spirit photographed the Lord Jesus from four varying viewpoints. Though He is the glorious subject of all four Gospels, each writer stressed a specific side of His personality, and so under inspiration selected materials that develop that particular trait." Does that statement agree with your concept of the Gospels? Does it help you understand their differences?

4. Were you surprised at the facts pointed out under the heading "In All Four Gospels" on page 20? Does Dr. Flynn's explanation on page 20 satisfy you?

2. How the Gospels Begin: The Gospel in the Genealogy

1. Had you ever noticed the similarity between Genesis 5:1 and Matthew 1:1 pointed out on page 25? What does this tell you about the relationship of the Old and New Testaments?

2. On page 26, Dr. Flynn summarizes the difference between Matthew's and Luke's handling of their lineage of Jesus: Discuss the ramifications of that dissimilarity.

3. Discuss the reasons why Tamar, Rahab, Ruth, and Bathsheba are included in Matthew's genealogy of Jesus.

4. What about the differences in each of these women's backgrounds?

5. Reread the last paragraph in this chapter. What does it say to you personally?

3. Only in Matthew

1. Reflect on the "three Major characteristics of the Gospel of Matthew: "Jewish, topical, kingly" on page 34. Discuss this in the light of the explanations that follow.

2. Look at the "miscellaneous links" on page 37*ff.* Do you agree with the author's conclusions? Can you think of other unique characteristics peculiar to Matthew?

3. Talk about creative ways to share the messiahship of Jesus with your Jewish friends and neighbors.

4. Flynn describes Matthew as an "accountant" on page 40. Why did his background make him the ideal reporter of the life of Christ for the Jews?

5. Reread the "Kingly" section beginning on page 40 and discuss the various aspects of Jesus' Kingship.

4. Who Is the King of Your Life?

1. As you think about the courage of the Romanian pastors described in the opening page of this chapter, consider what your own actions might have been in such circumstances and discuss.

2. Go through the same exercise in relation to the confrontation between Rome and the early Christians.

3. Reread and discuss Flynn's discussion of the use of time beginning on page 48.

4. Do the same for his discussions of "Money" and "Abilities." How do you "stack up" in these areas?

5. Repeat the exercise under "speech" and "ethical principles." Where does your "full allegiance" lie?

5. Only in Mark

1. Discuss the ramifications of Mark's key verse, 10:45 (see page 58).

2. Compare Mark's key words — Roman, busyness, and servanthood — to those of Matthew in Chapter 3.

3. Discuss Dr. Flynn's characterization of Peter as "a natural leader transformed from clay to rock" (p. 61). Based on your knowledge of Peter and his character, how would you describe him?

4. As you reread the section on "busyness," what is your impression of how Jesus lived once He began His public ministry (see pages 61-63)?

5. As you study the section on "servanthood" beginning on page 63, compare Jesus' role as a servant to the way many Christian leaders work today. Do you know any Christian leaders who are really "servants"?

6. Learning to Serve

1. At the beginning of this chapter, the author cites several lifestyle examples — Jimmy Carter, Hap Arnold, Samuel Brengle. Which of these men come closest to "living like Jesus" in your estimation?

2. Do you believe Christians today are concerned about status as were the Twelve as presented in the "Review the Teaching of Jesus" section beginning on page 73? Review and discuss.

3. How do you tell if a person is a servant leader (see page 76)?

4. Read the stories of Father Damien and the Elder on page 78. Apply their lessons to your own life and discuss their implications.

5. Read the story of the 40 seminarians beginning on page 79. With which group would you identify yourself?

7. Particularly in Luke

1. On page 83, the author uses three words to summarize Luke's Gospel: "Gentile, humanity, compassion." What do those words tell you about Jesus?

2. Dr. Flynn calls the Gospel of Luke "the portrait of a perfect man" (p. 84), who mixed toughness with tenderness. Discuss this portrait of Jesus.

3. What does the phrase "Son of Man" used by Luke to identify Jesus say to you about Him? Discuss.

4. On page 87, the author says that "Jesus was the perfect man, victorious where Adam had failed." Think about this truth and discuss.

5. Reread the section on "common human practices" on pages 89 to 91. How important are these "ingredients" to positive Christian living?

6. As you study the section on "compassion" beginning on page 91, reflect on the impact Christianity has had on today's

world. Where would our world be if it had not been for the "salt and light" influence of Christians down through the centuries?

8. It's Tough to Be Tender

1. On page 98, Dr. Flynn says that "even church members often lack sympathetic understanding." Do you agree with this assessment? Is this true of your church as a whole?

2. On page 99, the author describes what happened in a seminary class. Why is it usually difficult for "preachers" to "identify with the downtrodden"? Do you think this problem is widespread — or is it changing?

3. Using your "imagination" and "experience," look at some of the "irregular" people in your life. How does this exercise change your attitude toward that person or those persons?

4. Who do you think of when you read the story of Mary Reed on page 102?

5. Read the story of Dr. Robert McQuilkin on page 106. What does this tell you about priorities in life?

9. Uniquely in John

1. Read the key verse of John (16:28) in several translations and discuss the outline given on page 11. Does this better help you understand the uniqueness of this Gospel?

2. Read the first paragraph on page 113, and discuss the differences between John's view of Christ and that of Matthew.

3. In the "simplicity" section, beginning on page 114, Dr. Flynn describes Jesus as "the Father's message." Discuss the ramifications of that statement.

4. On page 115, Dr. Flynn says, "From Wedding (Cana) to grave (Bethany), Jesus is Master". What does this mean to you? Discover whether you agree or disagree with others in your group.

5. Look at the seven "I AM" statements on page 116 and 117 and think about those various aspects of Jesus' personality and ministry.

6. Discuss the concluding question in this chapter: "Just what does it mean to believe in Jesus?"

10. What It Means to Believe

1. Discuss the author's statement on page 124: "Flying a plane and becoming a Christian have a lot in common." How would you describe your conversion experience?

2. Have you ever had an experience like that described in the first paragraph on page 125? Is faith in another person or institution similar to what happens when one becomes a Christian?

3. Discuss the ramifications of the statement, "True Faith is not blind," on page 126. Read the author's discussion and put his argument in your own words.

4. "Faith is only as valid as its object," says the author on page 128. Discuss the implications of this statement. What are some examples of misplaced faith?

5. Read the section on "Committal" beginning on page 129ff. In the light of this discussion, what is your relationship to Christ?

11. In All Four Gospels: Barabbas and the Cross

1. Why do you think all four Gospels include the story of Barabbas?

2. Do you agree with the author's statement, "Barabbas is you"?

3. How do you react to the statement, "Barabbas was not awaiting trial, but execution"? Is that also true of us?

4. Had you ever thought of Barabbas as he is described in the sections on "Barabbas' Terror" and "Barabbas' Freedom"?

5. Reread the last paragraph/sentence in this chapter. Discuss its implications.

12. In All Four Gospels: The Empty Tomb

1. On page 148, Dr. Flynn writes: "To deny that the body of Christ rose, while at the same time affirming His resurrection, sounds like double-talk and smacks of intellectual dishonesty." Think about this statement and discuss.

2. Do you agree with the author that belief in the literal resurrection is pivotal to Christian faith?

3. Review the various "explanations" of the empty tomb on pages 151-155. Are any of these new to you? Why?

4. On page 156, Dr. Flynn quotes a missionary who said, "If they could find one bone of Jesus Christ, Christianity would fall to pieces." Do you agree? Why or why not?

5. Beginning on page 158 is the story of an atheist named Benham. Contrast his attitude toward death and that of the woman he met in the hospital. Reread his lament at the end of the story and contrast it with that of the woman.

6. Which "photograph" of Jesus (Matthew, Mark, Luke or John) is most meaningful to you as you look back at your study of *Four Faces of Jesus*?